THE STORY
OF THE STORY

HOW TO KIDNAP YOUR AUDIENCE

LAWRENCE J. KURNARSKY

This book is dedicated to

Ellie Partovi

Without her help, it would not have been written.

Also, many thanks to

Dennis Higgins, Mary Kenner & Dina and John
McAmmond

"We are, as a species, addicted to stories. Even when the body goes to sleep, the mind stays up all night, telling itself stories."

Jonathan Gottschall, *The Story Telling Animal: How Stories Make Us Human (*Mariner Books, *2013)*

PART I

BACKSTORY

1. Sea Change In Hollywood

After World War II, it was somehow decided that the USA was no longer bland enough. People, call them "folks," over-stimulated by too much harsh reality, were casting back to a more inane, simpler, if imaginary, past.

It was not just two wars and the Great Depression that had damaged the so-called American Way. While millions of men had been fighting overseas, women had been doing their jobs, and doing them well. When the men came back, there were not enough jobs.

Women needed to be retrofitted in angora sweaters. Coveralls were to be traded in for skirts hanging beneath the knees. Vivid colors were diluted to less stimulating pastels. Pointy ICBM bras were employed both to constrain and emphasize what was viewed as a gal's main function. Constraints were in order. A woman's place was in the home and she was expected to skedaddle back there and guard her virginity until after "Mr. Right" popped the question. Purity and Puritanism were considered as American as apple pie and were essential to the work ethic. Other notions about sex, gender roles, and alternative ways to live your life that ran counter to the prevailing doctrine, led to ruination. In the great land of individual liberty, conformity was now how you attained happiness.

There was also, thank God, Communism.

War production had ground to a stop and the Great Depression was returning as a sequel. It was The Commie Boogieman that allowed for a perpetual war economy. Like magic, factory chimneys began to belch black smoke again and the Depression ducked back around the corner. An era of prosperity was being ushered in, but it was being threatened. Unions and leftist intellectuals threatened prosperity. They had strayed from the righteous path. They questioned premises. Quite a few of the people questioning premises were storytellers. Some, who did their storytelling on the screen, had enormous influence. America and most of the world were hooked on the movies.

So, change came to Hollywood.

By the 1950s, there emerged in movies a new kind of storytelling emphasizing Clean, White, Conservative, Wholesome Conformity, and the Sexual Tease. The protagonists of the newer films were "decent," church going upholders of the American Way. What the "American Way" was, Americans were expected to know –the way in war films a soldier returning from behind enemy lines was expected to instantly rattle off who the starting pitchers were in the 1928 World Series. Hesitation risked being shot. That was The American Way. You questioned not its premises.

2. Before And After

The stubble-bearded protagonists of many of the best-loved noir films of the era between the great wars tended to be outsiders who "knew the score" and who had decided not to play the game. Naiveté was presented in these films as needing a cure, but the innocent still needed protecting. These heroes remained righteous, if cynical, even reluctant, champions of the weak against the strong. They understood that there would be a price to pay for their heroism. Of course, if they did change sides, they knew that life could become much easier. There had to be the choice for the outsiders to come in from the cold, or they would not be heroes. But coming in from the cold usually meant moral compromise. **The golden thread of morality was stretched in these protagonists to where it just might break.** Yet, in the end, it usually did not, and perhaps it could not.

The characters in the screwball comedies during the hungry Thirties and early Forties brought levity to millions, but the protagonists in these films tended to be nothing if not lovable eccentrics. There was almost always something wacky about them that linked to something rare and incorruptible. They were not normal. **Love of the oddball, the rule breaker, and the questioner is in the DNA of these quintessentially American comic movies.** To be different invited social sanction, but happiness required you to find your own way and, unlike many of the noir thrillers, these zany protagonists earned a happy ending.

The cowboy hero of the Hollywood Western often could not even live indoors. He was an outsider –literally– comfortable only when sleeping under the stars. "Town" meant constraints on freedom. "Town" was tainted and an obvious substitution for "society." When the cowboy rode into town, he met folks who "didn't cotton much to strangers," and he definitely was one –even if he grew up there.

The cowboy hero was too evolved to endure society for long. It did not help that the "good town-folk" were deluded enough to think that it was not him but the banker or the Cattleman's Association who represented virtue. The town-folk had it upside-down. That was normal. That is why, when the cowboy rode into town, it was for a bath, a woman (briefly) and provisions. If he lingered, it was often because of the torch he still carried for the grocer's or the sheriff's wife.

That lady, of course, still loved him, but she had opted for "town."

If the cowboy stayed too long, he became ensnared in the corruption of the town. He was morally bound to protect the town from the outlaws, whose boss often wore a pinstriped suit as bosses often did during that era. The sheriff was rarely up to the task. If he was not on the boss's payroll, he was cowed by him, tamed by "town." After saving the town, if he survived, the cowboy rode off into the sunset.

To fight on behalf of those who reject you was in the job description for the Hollywood heroes of this era. It was standard in these stories to equate "outsider" with virtue and "insider" with moral taint.

That script flipped when Joe McCarthy and his House Committee for Un-American Activities (HUAC) boys rode into Tinsel Town. After that, the journey was increasingly back to, not away from, normality. Normal became "the good." The natural hierarchy of winners and losers was, well, natural. It was beyond question. Hollywood heroes morphed into clean-shaven, square-jawed, company men—more likely to be cops than private eyes. They guarded against those who strayed off the straight and narrow.

In many of the mainstream movies made after Mc-Carthy, hard work and fair play are rewarded. You would want to stay with the firm in these stories. Any woman a company man would marry would want no more than to make him happy and raise his babies. She was delighted to be in a supporting role. Women were viewed as biologically driven to serve and nurture. The kitchen, the store, and the beauty parlor were their turf. If they had money, the opera, the social club, and the dinner party were their turf. Men were driven by complementary instincts with an emphasis on the urge to make money and to protect. The streets, the battlefield, and the office were their turf.

The standard issue movie hero of the previous era can play the game, but, if he does, at some plot point he chooses to leave. Make no mistake about it, this is to preserve his soul. That is made very clear in movies like The Treasure of the Sierra Madre. If the protagonist gives in to the game and tries to be like everyone else, he summons demons, and the ending is tragic. The Treasure of the Sierra Madre was made in 1948 –just before McCarthy came blazing into Hollywood– and so it shares the DNA of the earlier period.

Most Hollywood storytellers before McCarthy understood all was not right in Oz. They assumed that often –maybe usually– bad people win and good people are ground under their heels. The difference can be summed up with two opposing social views. Before the sea change, the apple barrel was depicted as contaminated with rotten apples with the unspoiled ones risking contagion. World War II ends, the "good guys" win, and quite suddenly, the apples in the barrel are doing fine thank you very much. It is the odd rotten apple that threatens the bunch. It is the outsider who is the threat.

With a few exceptions, Americans, alas, fell victim to the manufactured psychology of the moment. They drank the Kool-Aid. There was little blowback. There was almost a sense of relief as the movies departed from reflecting the way it is to creating the Norman Rockwell illusion of how we would like the world to be – meaning how McCarthy and his gang wanted it to be.

I am not thinking of those great classic Hollywood movies that provide a means for escaping the humdrum of the daily routine and life's pesky trials and tribulations. There had always been escapist movies like that. **The difference is that these new movies seemed to advocate escape from the truth of things, which is like trying to escape the callings of your own soul. These new style movies, TV shows, and even some books were soulless in a way few movies, even bad movies, had been before.**

Many professional writers, actors, and directors were painfully aware that nothing less than the integrity of storytelling itself was under attack, but most feared for their careers and, since it was still the era of the Hollywood studio system, those who wanted to work tended to complain only to trusted friends and family. In public and at work, they chose to grin and bear it. The Hollywood bosses, who formerly had been inconsistent in defending their creative employees, now jumped on the HUAC bandwagon and became intolerant of the slightest hint of dissent. The diminishing power of the unions was, of course, a welcome bonus for the studio execs, for obvious reasons. For one thing, it meant they could grind down salaries and pay rates. It has to be added however, in the studios defense, that because of the "new media" at that time, television, it had become considerably more difficult for a studio release to make a buck. You might

Post-McCarthy Hollywood is an Oz where winners deserve to win, losers deserve to lose, and the wizard really is a wizard –in fact, he might be God.

3. What Endured And What Endures In Hollywood

It's Called Show "Business" For a Reason.

Before the McCarthyite purge, the creatives often were at odds with the Hollywood "suits," but it was the take at the box-office that settled whether they would get a paycheck or not. But, when McCarthy added an ideological litmus test, even Charlie Chaplin had to high tail it out of town.

Some big names fought back successfully, yet they had huge box-office clout. Bogart told Joe where to stuff it. Generally though, Hollywood creatives kept a low profile. If summoned to testify, they gave up as few names as possible in exchange for a career. Names though, were given. Many talented, good people suffered unemployment and indignity. A few really had been communists, but most had only been antiauthoritarian freethinkers which had been a proud American tradition. It was probably this tradition that non-Americans most admired about the USA. There was conformity and rigidity enough in the "old country."

Good movies were still made after the sea change, some of the best. There were reasons. Hollywood was in a fight with television and needed to up the quality. And, of course, you can't keep a good writer down. Creativity finds ways. Even so, something profound had changed.

In many of the mainstream movies made after Mc-Carthy, hard work and fair play are rewarded. You would want to stay with the firm in these stories. Any woman a company man would marry would want no more than to make him happy and raise his babies. She was delighted to be in a supporting role. Women were viewed as biologically driven to serve and nurture. The kitchen, the store, and the beauty parlor were their turf. If they had money, the opera, the social club, and the dinner party were their turf. Men were driven by complementary instincts with an emphasis on the urge to make money and to protect. The streets, the battlefield, and the office were their turf.

The standard issue movie hero of the previous era can play the game, but, if he does, at some plot point he chooses to leave. Make no mistake about it, this is to preserve his soul. That is made very clear in movies like The Treasure of the Sierra Madre. If the protagonist gives in to the game and tries to be like everyone else, he summons demons, and the ending is tragic. The Treasure of the Sierra Madre was made in 1948 –just before McCarthy came blazing into Hollywood– and so it shares the DNA of the earlier period.

Most Hollywood storytellers before McCarthy understood all was not right in Oz. They assumed that often –maybe usually– bad people win and good people are ground under their heels. The difference can be summed up with two opposing social views. Before the sea change, the apple barrel was depicted as contaminated with rotten apples with the unspoiled ones risking contagion. World War II ends, the "good guys" win, and quite suddenly, the apples in the barrel are doing fine thank you very much. It is the odd rotten apple that threatens the bunch. It is the outsider who is the threat.

With a few exceptions, Americans, alas, fell victim to the manufactured psychology of the moment. They drank the Kool-Aid. There was little blowback. There was almost a sense of relief as the movies departed from reflecting the way it is to creating the Norman Rockwell illusion of how we would like the world to be – meaning how McCarthy and his gang wanted it to be.

I am not thinking of those great classic Hollywood movies that provide a means for escaping the humdrum of the daily routine and life's pesky trials and tribulations. There had always been escapist movies like that. **The difference is that these new movies seemed to advocate escape from the truth of things, which is like trying to escape the callings of your own soul. These new style movies, TV shows, and even some books were soulless in a way few movies, even bad movies, had been before.**

Many professional writers, actors, and directors were painfully aware that nothing less than the integrity of storytelling itself was under attack, but most feared for their careers and, since it was still the era of the Hollywood studio system, those who wanted to work tended to complain only to trusted friends and family. In public and at work, they chose to grin and bear it. The Hollywood bosses, who formerly had been inconsistent in defending their creative employees, now jumped on the HUAC bandwagon and became intolerant of the slightest hint of dissent. The diminishing power of the unions was, of course, a welcome bonus for the studio execs, for obvious reasons. For one thing, it meant they could grind down salaries and pay rates. It has to be added however, in the studios defense, that because of the "new media" at that time, television, it had become considerably more difficult for a studio release to make a buck. You might

Hollywood had been tamed, and it still has not entirely come back.

This, then, was when I think the mechanic's view of writing became legitimated, when themes became memes, and when scriptwriters started mixing and matching clichés about characters – dressing them like paper dolls and shunting them through a snakes-and-ladders second act to arrive in the final act pretty much where the audience had figured they were going. These movies might have been artfully made, but were, proudly, almost patriotically, not art. Art was for foreigners (outsiders) and eggheads (outsiders).

Studio heads always tended to view movies as a commodity, but now this notion began to corrupt "above-the-line" creative Hollywood. **Quite suddenly in movies, attaining happiness became less of a difficult pursuit and more easily fulfilled by conforming.** Big Questions were for church. Decent folk stuck with the answers they had been given. Thinking too much –or worse, reading –could get you into hot water, lead to depression, and generally lead you astray. You could become an outsider, which meant you could not be truly happy. Worse, you could become a danger to the happiness of everyone else. And, sometimes, reading could lead to glasses! Glasses in many (rightfully forgotten) Cold War movies were a red flag.

It would be nice to be able to claim that most Americans felt, viscerally, a loss in the quality of storytelling and were righteously offended at the loss of the freedom to test conventions because that had been part of traditional storytelling in the USA. But there were no mobs armed with pitchforks and torches marching on Hollywood.

say the Hollywood big-wigs had been blind-sided twice: once by Joe McCarthy and HUAC, and then by the sudden appearance of television which was free –sorta. Free except for the plague of ads.

4. The Significance Of The Sea Change

We are not really talking about politics here but about something deeper that underlies politics, as well as every other aspect of life. **The job of storytelling can be described as the controlled revelation of what is significant on the human journey.** That is something every storyteller should be clear on and know in his or her bones. This makes all the difference.

It has been said many times that science exists to answer the question "what," while art is concerned with the question "why." Especially arts like poetry and storytelling, but arguably all art, are obsessively concerned with the "why" of it all. **Our task is not to comfort audiences or readers but to wake them up to meaning.** If waking them up also comforts them, so be it. It will not always. To do the job at all, storytellers need to be ruthlessly honest with themselves and courageous in the attempt to honestly get through to their readers and audiences. **What needs to be gotten through is nothing less than the meaning of life**.

Although storytelling is not politics, having a political point of view, or a philosophical or religious bias, is unavoidable. You can really only write from your own point of view –especially if what you want to really bag is meaning. The job, therefore, is not to convince readers and audiences to adopt your particular politics or philosophy but to get at what truth underlies your convictions. Hopefully, your truth will connect with theirs. The more your truth intersects with the lives of others, the more you will succeed –and the more money you will probably make.

You need to write from conviction to be a good storyteller. Even if you write someone else's story, you need to make it your own. Considering the immensity of the project of telling even the simplest tale well, storytelling cannot be chained to ideology but rather to the internal battle of human virtue with human vice.

The audience and readers between the "World Wars" preferred their life truths straight up, no chaser. Audiences have probably liked their stories that way since pretty much forever but –with the notable exception of classical Greece (from which we get the word "drama") until roughly the time of Shakespeare– the truths conveyed through stories tended to be handed down from storyteller to storyteller to be taken on faith by the unwashed masses. The stories in the Bible are like that: they are to be taken as true. Taken, that is, as an article of faith. Modern storytelling, however, puts the burden on the storyteller to, in a sense, must prove the case.

With modernism and growing scientific knowledge, faith began to falter. It became necessary to question those truths and prove them in stories with **protagonists who filled in for the audience as the test takers and antagonists, and whose job it was to do the testing.** That process is how a story becomes credible and hopefully gripping.

Audiences do not shy away from the truth about life, even when it is a prickly truth, if it holds their attention and strikes them as credible. In fact, they usually delight in taking that storytelling journey, no matter how peril-ous, **if the imaginary hero's journey intersects with what they face in their real lives.**

Those are not insignificant "ifs," but if the master skill for storytellers is the art of controlled revelation –reve-lation implies that there is something worth revealing at the end of the process. **Honesty and courage are nec-essary for a storyteller to pull off the trick. Honesty and courage are needed to take on the conventional, comfortable, complacent, and familiar.** This means that every storyteller must, to some degree, be an out-sider, and the same thing can be said about every story hero. The degree of discomfort the audience or readers are being confronted with by the characters and events can vary, but if the common understanding of "what is" collides with the storyteller's assessment of "what is," it is the storyteller's moral duty to raise the challenge not through intellectual argument but through drama, through the hero's journey. That journey is, each and ev-ery time, toward meaning and true value.

That was the sacred trust that came under assault in the artificially glib era following World War II. During that era, if a story did not coincide with the "common under-standing," the errant black sheep storyteller would be culled from the flock and ritually, publicly, slaughtered. The crusade was led by a mad true believer named Joe McCarthy who was intent on burning witches on an altar of frenzied, ultra-patriotic sanctimony, which is the way it always happens.

Obviously, no human being is capable of grasping the complete truth, meaning, and significance of any-thing; but being honest in the attempt is what counts. Without honesty and artistic integrity, insight is

impossible. Without delivering insight, there is no true storytelling, just pageants and miracle plays, as there had been, for the most part, during the Dark Ages. Miracle plays and pageants relied on two-dimensional biblical characters that everyone knew, mechanically pushed through plots that everyone also knew. Does that sound familiar? Have you seen any movies or TV shows like that?

The plots and characters for miracle plays were cribbed from the Bible, and the themes and premises were sanctioned by the Church and political authorities. No one could openly challenge their themes or premises without taking a serious risk. The risk was being found guilty of heresy. The consequence of merely being charged could be torture on the rack, and the sentence for being found guilty was often being burnt at the stake. After McCarthy, the risk was also significantly greater than what storytellers in America ever had to face, but the tie in to the pre-modern past was –as they said in classical Hollywood, a natural.

At bottom, those who dared to stand up to McCarthy were defending the right to question values –including the common consensus– if it was in pursuit of truth and meaning. What they were being accused of, by HUAC, was heresy.

But, here is the problem: heresy of this kind is unavoidable if you want to tell a good story. In every second act of every honest story, premises and themes are made to run the gauntlet. They need to be "proven" by the writer to make them credible to the audience. The skilled storyteller contrives to goad the audience into feeling skeptical about the characters and the outcomes. This is part of showing you, rather than just telling you, that something is true as they do in a Miracle Play and, here we go, as McCarthy demanded storytellers to do. In a properly told story, themes and premises laid down in Act I either are left standing by the end of Act II or lie bloodied and dead for all to see. Either way, the audience has viscerally traveled along with the protagonist through the trials and tribulations of Act II. The audience experiences the story emotionally, not just intellectually. By Act III, the audience understands why the story turned out the way it did.

Watching a miracle play or pageant is simply not the same. It is the difference between propaganda and art.

Luckily, the days of pageants and miracle plays were numbered. Unluckily, it was a large number. Like Sleeping Beauty, the art of the story had been laid out in a glass coffin, seemingly dead, until approximately the 14th century when Sleeping Beauty was reawakened with the kiss of a prince, a Greek prince. For the rebirth of the story, not to mention science, occurs largely as a consequence of Greek thinking and drama being reintroduced into Europe via Moorish Spain. It would be late in the 14th century that the wonderfully naughty and insightful Canterbury Tales appears. The year was 1386 –about a millennium after the fall of Rome. Chaucer brilliantly does this in a biblical disguise. The setting is a pilgrimage. In the 20th century –confronted by a not entirely dissimilar repression– American writers would do something similar in the guise of a cowboy Western. The setting might be a cattle drive.

We call the era after Rome fell the Dark Ages for a reason. I make the comparison with McCarthy's hordes sacking Hollywood for a reason.

This is not to say that there was not wisdom and abiding truth in some Dark Ages tales, but there was also a lot of bunk and hokum. By bunk and hokum, I do not refer to flights of the storyteller's imagination. I refer to elements in stories that make no sense or contradict experience. I refer to premises and values that are to be taken as articles of faith. When what is bunk and hokum is not allowed to be separated from what is real and true, storytelling is out the window. That impedes the storyteller's right and duty to be honest. (The audience, of course, has no reciprocating duty to like the writer's story.)

America's greatest and most loved writer of humor, Samuel Clemens (better known by his nom de plume, Mark Twain), separated the bunk and hokum from the truth as well as any writer ever has, and there is little doubt that he would have been blacklisted by McCarthy if his death fifty years earlier had not cheated the witch burner. The efforts of puffed-up, bigoted, self-righteous buffoons to bury morality under their insufferable moralism was diametrically opposed to his life's work.

It is incumbent, as much on storytellers as on scientists, to delineate between what we might want to believe and what is, in fact, our situation. It is their stock-in-trade to offer insight –whether into war, love, or the humdrum daily routines of everyday people. Yet, in the Fifties there emerged an attempt to do the very thing that this bunch of throwbacks were accusing many writers of doing –to socially engineer beliefs with the explicit aim of propagating an ideology. Their idiotic crusade against what they considered alien ideologies threatening The American Way took precedence over writing about what is authentic, significant, and real in the human journey.

This was a breathtakingly narrow-minded redefinition of what it means to be an "American."

And the thing is, these self-righteous, patriot buffoons just about pulled it off.

All of a sudden, there were sanctioned truths beyond questioning. We were heading back to an era of miracle plays. They wanted storytelling to serve as the LIGHT against the DARKNESS, in capital letters. It was now to be a battle that took place outside the main characters rather than within them. It was now us as angels against them as devils.

That tendency has always existed, but it had been recognized from at least the age of Shakespeare as a sign of weak storytelling.

The need for honest conviction as a storyteller explains why the protagonists of even pot-boiler thrillers and screwball comedies of the Thirties and Forties were cut from a different cloth than the standard one-dimensional characters of pageants and miracle plays –let alone the clean-shaven protagonists and heroes of the propagandistic era following World War II. After all, the modern novel was born only a hundred and some years before Hollywood started churning out movies. There was a lot of literary talent working for the studios in the Thirties and Forties. Some of them, like Raymond Chandler, were downright ashamed of it, but the money was good.

Perhaps that is why classic Hollywood heroes were sometimes portrayed as readers and always as thinkers. There was forethought and back-story behind their decisions and actions. There was a sense, even a painful sense, of free will. Free will is depicted as a gift but also a burden. Most hardboiled noir heroes were portrayed as psychological wrecks –down on their luck and un-comfortable in their own skins– largely because of this burden of honesty and consciousness. (Hamlet, a failed hero, also had this problem.) This is why the noir pro-tagonists usually had more in common with the losers of the era than the winners –preferring the company of hobos and drunks to ministers and bankers.

That said, these Hollywood heroes were not rabble-rous-ers. They were never overtly political, but they could be politicians –as in Frank Capra's much-loved Mr. Smith Goes to Washington. In this movie, Jimmy Stewart por-trays a reluctant senator as an affable, unassuming fel-low who is no "everyman." To the contrary, Mr. Smith is an extraordinary man –clever, kind, courageous, honest, and in love with liberty and democracy. He is, therefore, a true American hero and, according to Capra, an an-ti-politician. The portrayal, of course, is utter fiction, and a still popular fiction in politics today.

The point is, Mr. Smith was not the kind of "American Hero" a real Senator, Joe McCarthy, believed in. A few years after this film was made, Frank Capra would be ac-cused of being a communist propagandist by HUAC.

But it was HUAC who were the political propagandists. These Golden Era characters were, and remain, portray-als of authentic American heroes – by which I mean, post Enlightenment heroes who embodied in fiction what is most noble and fine in the fragmented American psyche. These heroes were never true-believers and could never be. They were painfully aware of the tragic-comedy tak-ing place around them. Their honesty was built in, and they lacked the usual filters. As a result, they were skep-tics, usually miserably so, except when they fell for some gal. And that normally would end badly. Disappointment was inevitable for this kind of hero. But they kept their pain and their doubts mostly to themselves, until a plot point when they no longer could. Quite often this plot point coincided with when they were the most drunk. "Most drunk" often equates in these movies with "most lost." Good writers, after all, write about what they know.

These were heroes wracked with doubt, who faced crises of faith with depressing regularity. Of course, faith was not what it used to be after World War I and the Great Depression. These were dark times, and its heroes were equipped in the darkness with only the flicker of a match to light a cigarette and guide their way. Readers or audiences identified with them because, at bottom, they faced the same demons and similar challenges. This is how it always has to be with effective storytelling.

If the vitriol of these kinds of protagonists comes out directly at all, it is in pain, often in the throes of drunken semi-coherent rants. It was always personal, and almost never overtly political. The audience, at the time, nevertheless got the message because it jived with their own experience. Depression-era audiences understood that survival meant you needed to question authority. As it was in the movies, so also in daily life: you cannot trust someone simply because of the cut of the suit or because he or she is considered a pillar of the community. The pillars of the community in the movies of this era, as in life, often preyed on the community. Even that most American of suppositions –that in the end, you work hard and you get what you deserve– is laid out on the examination table in the best of these stories. **It follows, then, that the virtuous in these stories get their teeth knocked out with some regularity.**

Hollywood storytelling between the wars dovetailed with common experience and common understanding, and that led to the enormous popularity of Hollywood noir. That is exactly what goaded the anti-communist crusaders who had emerged from the woodwork after World War II. They recoiled from the common understanding. They put much of the blame for the common understanding on storytellers, and so they resolved to change the stories. That meant turning the truth inside out and upside down, but they could not have cared less, and, what is more, they largely succeeded. A great many of their "fellow American Patriots" joined their crusade.

And so it was that, in the late Forties, a schism began to emerge between reality and how most people experienced reality as well as what was portrayed in movies and books. Politics aside, that change was not simply a swing back to portraying a more conservative and conventional take on life. It was an about-face from the literary traditions of at least four centuries. This was, to say the least, a radical change.

5. Schism

Hollywood movies of the Thirties and Forties, including quite a few that displeased the House Un-American Activities Committee, were not a departure from the Western storytelling traditions that predated them. To the contrary, they were consistent with storytelling in Shakespeare's 17th century plays, the 18th century novels of Cervantes and Fielding, the 19th century works of Hugo, Dickens, Hardy, Melville, Tolstoy and Twain, and, so on, into the 20th century. There was no communist plot to dupe American audiences even if quite a few of the most successful Hollywood writers, such as Dashiell Hammett or Dalton Trumbo were politically of the left.

Even in light romantic fantasy –what we can call fluff– such as the happily trite Busby Berkeley dance films, the stories remained what they always had been about: characters in pursuit of life's essential truths. **These fundamental truths were spun into themes introduced in Act I; tested through the trials and tribulations visited upon the protagonists by the antagonists in Act II; and the results delivered in Act III.**

The means of passing the tests of Act II were also what they had always been: choosing to exercise virtues such as generosity, kindness, courage, honesty, and forgiveness – or the consequences of failing to do what is right. Doing what is right, of course, is not simply following the moral precepts that you are taught. In fact, it can never be that simple or easy, for a story worth telling. That a protagonist chooses virtue over selfishness is what makes for heroism, even if it is not what makes for a happy ending. Certainly, the popular audience of the Dirty Thirties understood that happy endings are not guaranteed in life either. They were prepared to accept any ending if it were made credible. Storytellers understood, for their part, that a sad ending must not be an unsatisfactory ending.

It is not that readers and audiences of this period, or any other, hoped for a sad ending. The endings of classic movies of that time, such as The Treasure of The Sierra Madre, The Big Sleep, or, later, High Noon, undoubtedly were not what the audience desired for the protagonists, since they would not want that for themselves. But these films were huge hits –sad or happy endings notwithstanding– and this kind of storytelling was entirely consistent with the best plays and novels of any era. If it was radical, blame it on people like Shakespeare and Cervantes.

It was the turn-away from the storytelling tradition that, in reality, attempted to reframe facing real life as a radical act. The anti-communist ideologues of HUAC were, in fact, the storytelling revisionists and the actual radical idealists. No matter what the personal take on life is, every writer needs to present his or her case through comedy or tragedy, using fantasy, satire, romance, mystery, adventure, social realism –whatever the vehicle– and then prove the case in front of jurors we call audiences or the readership by Act III. That is how it had been, and how it must be. It has little to nothing to do with ideology, and the best writers always know this even if Senator McCarthy and his gang begged to differ.

Virtue is at the core of storytelling, its absence or its presence. Under their tough crust, Hollywood heroes of the Golden Era were rarely idealists; never true-believers; but almost always, free thinking, kind-hearted skeptics who were burdened, as much as aided, by their moral compasses.

Virtue was being assessed and measured in their stories, as it should be in your story.

It is as impossible to imagine an idealist Bogart protagonist, as it is a Bogart protagonist who, at core, is selfish or cowardly, even if he would like to give that impression; even if, like Bogart's character in The African Queen, the decision to finally do what is right is not an easy one to make. Why should it be easy? If it was easy, that would put both the clergy and storytellers out of a job.

Virtue, though, is not something a skeptic wears on his sleeve. The protagonists of the classic era of American movie making do not broadcast their virtues. (Modesty is, after all, a virtue.) Most often they hide who they really are from others, with less success from those who know them or love them –and with even less success, from themselves. Many of the protagonists of this era attempt to drown their sorrows in a bottle. They are entirely human. But their true character is revealed through the action in Act II.

Notice, please, the distinction between their "true character" that is revealed, versus their "true nature." This is a distinction worth making. **If deeds are governed by someone's "nature" rather than through the exercise of free will, there can be no true hero, nor, for that matter, no true villain since the characters would then be operating on autopilot.** Many of the protagonists depicted in popular culture after World War II were, at core, automatons: heroes by disposition rather than by free will. They are not motivated by a moral core, but governed by it.

The two laconic cop protagonists of the hugely successful TV series, Dragnet, are prime examples of protagonists who run on autopilot. Not only is there no inner conflict – there is no inner life. I suppose there is a kind of morbid fascination, akin to eating junk food, in watching life unfold as it should: the good guys meting out justice to the bad guys, as if it's inevitable that virtue wins out over vice, as if it's credible that the matter is settled in one episode or one film. Inevitability puts the kibosh on audience interest. **Central characters, particularly protagonists, need an inner life. It is important for you, as a storyteller, to get that across, and to toss in**

a good measure of inner conflict reflecting the outer conflict in Act II.

The art of implying an inner life is a necessary challenge for both filmmaking and film acting. The depiction of an inner life is more natural to the novel form since psychology can be directly conveyed through words. That is a major strength, perhaps the major strength, of the novel. A movie, however, is primarily a visual art form. Television lies in between. **The story in a movie is conveyed through the tension between what the audience sees happening on the screen and what they are hearing characters say.**

There are plenty of wonderful dialog driven movies from the Thirties, Forties, and early Fifties, like Grand Hotel or His Girl Friday, but words do not suffice for even these films. This is one reason why most movie heroes between the wars, and to this day, prove themselves more through deeds than words –certainly more than Shakespeare's verbose protagonists do. But it is more than that. "Actions speak louder than words," and "a picture is worth a thousand words." A movie protagonist needs to show the audience who he or she really is through action. This proof is on the screen. What you see on a stage when attending a play simply cannot compare.

Perhaps, since it is protagonists rather than antagonists who need to prove their mettle before the movie audience, on the screen the tradition has developed that most of the good lines are spoken by villains. In the movies as in comic books, villainy and verbosity often go together.

A general tendency favoring action over verbosity is about all the protagonists during the years between World War I and World War II have in common with the squeaky clean, politically sanitized, mindless-conformist characters in many of the movies and TV shows made in the period after. Leave It to Beaver, Bewitched, and The Brady Bunch are emblematic of that period. Normalcy is more than desirable. It is almost a fetish. (Especially in Bewitched.) Anyone straying from the norm is either a comic character, usually in a supporting role, or, if it is a protagonist, he or she had better grow up fast.

The implication is that there is something wrong and threatening about people who are "different." "Grow up," in this context, means that the prodigal son or daughter must return to the conformist fold. The "fold" or the "herd" is where you are fulfilled and protected. What you are protected from, at bottom, is abnormality. The hero protagonists of these kinds of stories act as armed shepherds of the flock –that is, as strong, tough, righteous, conservative father figures.

That formula, placed on its head, is how normalcy had been portrayed in many pre-McCarthy era movies like High Noon, in which the flock, meaning society, ends up cowardly betraying the cowboy hero. The cowboy hero is pretty much on his own when he saves the town – the town being the community that stands in for our society, and therefore for all of us chickens.

Gary Cooper does his job, but he will never join town again. He leaves town with his wife, portrayed by the ethereal Grace Kelly, to set up a ranch very far away from this town and, needless to say, probably from any town. But now, at least, he will have a companion other than his horse and a roof over his head. At least there is that much hope.

For Sam Spade, or Philip Marlowe, battle weary private eyes in noir classics like The Maltese Falcon and The Big Sleep, normalcy would do nothing to cure what ails them or what ails the city in which they ply their shadowy trade. The status quo is corrupt and every new day on the job reaffirms the notion that bullies normally get what they want. It is virtue embodied only by a few that staves off utter decadence.

These kinds of noir heroes chose to leave the preaching to preachers. They were, however, careful listeners by disposition and profession. Sure, they were tough and street smart, but they also had inferred complex, uneasy interior lives. Perhaps that is what happens when you "call a spade a spade," when you are willing to stare into the abyss. **These hard-boiled, reluctant heroes fully understood that virtue is more often punished than it is rewarded. When virtue is rewarded in one of these tales, therefore, the reward is painfully earned. This is necessary to make the hero's journey meaningful.**

6. Getting Back To The Job Of Revealing Meaning

Revealing what is meaningful in life is the destination for all good tales. The movies from Hollywood's Golden Era tended to put on trial the common consensus in order to do just that, to distinguish between what we might want to believe is meaningful and true, and what is meaningful and true. These writers of fiction took on the big questions of life because that is what you do to tell a good tale. Of course, this is no hard science. Every story is but an approximation. These writers wanted to at least describe a course to what is important for human beings in life. All good writers make the same attempt. The audience or readers decide how well they have succeeded.

The mission is not just to hold audience interest, but to hold their interests as you reveal something of the truth about life's journey.

Genre is irrelevant to that mission. Whether comedy, farce, romance, action-adventure, thriller, western, or science fiction, they all must take on fundamental issues related to personal and human happiness. Like Old Testament Jacob they attempt to wrestle angels to the ground; and also like Old Testament Jacob, they can never ultimately win. It is as true for writing fiction, as it is with living life: It is not the destination; it is the journey that matters most. All good writers and all good directors know that.

So how do we get there? **Honesty is a core value for heroes and the same must hold true for their storytellers, at least when facing the blank page**. Honesty and clarity of vision characterized the best storytelling of the period referred to as the Golden Age of Hollywood. These protagonists might be mentally exhausted, temporarily beaten down, seemingly at the end of their ropes; but they could not be fooled, not for long. When it was time to act in the cause of virtue, they acted. It is almost inevitable that these protagonists, as they go through the travails of Act II, convey within the subtext a social critique at odds with what might be called the official version of reality.

It seems inevitable that there would be blow-back from those who felt that the villains of these stories were them in thin disguise. The world's greatest novelists, with their stories, incurred similar wrath. They were unafraid of attacking the smug, rich, powerful, or comfortable. (For this crime, Victor Hugo was sent into exile.) They were unafraid of targeting anyone, or any class, that seemed to warrant being attacked. It was all in the effort to get at the truth.

It would be wrong to assume that there were more fans of the politically correct movies made after HUAC did its damage than during the decades before. In other words, it is wrong to assume that American audiences were just waiting to embrace what HUAC wanted to offer them. The movies made according to the HUAC family recipe were neither more popular, nor more profitable than what had come before. If audience buy-in is to be the metric, the audience adored what McCarthy and gang considered questionably patriotic movies such as The Wizard of Oz and The Grapes of Wrath, lavishing on Hollywood reams and reams of cash. The pre-World War II movies, including those condemned by the committee, were made inside Hollywood's factory studio system. Money had been the producer's main motive (nothing un-American about that) and so the Hollywood bigshots could not have been more delighted. During the worst years of the Great Depression, Beverly Hills mansions and Duesenberg cars were selling like hot cakes. (A Duesenberg could cost up to $20,000 in a time when a tuna sandwich might cost fifteen cents.)

HUAC was right about one thing: some of the biggest box-office hits of the Thirties and Forties were subversive. They subverted the complacent idea that, at center, everything is okay in the good ol' USA. That was in direct opposition to the post World War Two patriotic comforting notion that social decay was being fomented by exterior forces. The noir thrillers of the Golden Era left the impression that corruption is, and always had been, woven into the fabric of American life. To put it bluntly, these movies ripped holes in the American Dream. They pointed to hypocrisy, unfairness, and inequality as a significant part of the American reality. And American audiences were anything but offended. World War I and the economic collapse that occurred a little more than a decade later left huge cracks in the common consensus of what the country really was. People were losing faith in their leaders and the promises they were making.

The best storytellers were going to take advantage of this breakdown of the common consensus, because they were driven to get at the truth and this was an opportunity. If that meant shattering illusions, so be it. After all, if you were a noir hero, skepticism kept you from getting a bullet in the back of the head.

Or we might put it this way: The common consensus needed to be fractured to allow in the light.

That needs to be underscored: Hypocrisy, unfairness, and inequality were common then and still are. This is pretty much the case everywhere, not just in the USA, but including in the USA.

This is also true: the best writers and storytellers of the classical era tried, through various plots, fanciful social satire like The Wizard of Oz, and even direct social criticism such as Preston Sturges' Sullivan's Travels, not to destroy America, but to find it.

 It was, and is, all a means to an end. The idea of storytelling is to shed light on what truly is important and meaningful in the human journey. Storytellers rely on the cracks in the fabric of the grand Illusion to get at the big questions in life. **All of those Big Questions can be summed up as: given what we humans are up against, how do we find honor and happiness?**

You need to know what you are up against if you do not want to be a chump, do not you?

Heroes cannot be chumps. Chumps are gullible. Chumps fall for the official story hook, line, and sinker. The noir heroes, between the wars, usually were as much at odds with the cops as with the crooks, partly because they were the opposite of gullible. They were painfully aware. They were interested in the contents, not the packaging. In their world of shadows, there were both good and bad people, and they could be found anywhere, including in the shadows. Noir protagonists have friends or enemies on both sides, and one could turn into the other as the plots thickened. It was not appearances, or what you did for a living that counted, but how you did it and who you did it to. It was not what you were before, but what you were now that mattered. It was the contents of your character. Everyone had their reasons and their back story.

This was not a simple world. It was never neat and tidy. It is not a simple world. It is never neat and tidy. Integrity was, and is, difficult to maintain. Despite inhabiting a world of shadows, protagonists, especially of noir films, were prone to see clearly. It was as much a curse as a gift. They smoked too many cigarettes and drank too much cheap booze as a means of self-medication. (Much like too many writers do.)

It cost them, but they knew this: people do not always get what they deserve. Justice is not guaranteed. Freedom demands sacrifice. Sometimes you need to take on the institutions that are supposed to be on your side. Thus, art imitated life in Hollywood between the wars. Corruption was often portrayed as systemic because, sorry, that was just what was going on. The threat to happiness was understood to be as much inside as outside. You did not get to choose. It was not one or the other. It was both.

What changed after World War II was that there was a direct attempt to make life imitate art, and to control art. After McCarthy, movies became more polemical and propagandistic, not less. That is just the way it was.

And so, a new sanitized hero was created, like a Frankenstein. The hero's journey also changed. The journey was now to social acceptance. The hero was an insider, who proudly believed what his country wanted him to believe. Alternatively, the hero began as outsider, who could have turned out badly, but learned to be an insider and became good. This hero won the day, damsel, and the happy-ever-after, by conforming to and protecting what was called normal. And you had better believe that normal was good.

This was storytelling from the outside, rather than the inside. It was the packaging, rather than what was in the box, and I cannot say it less than blatantly: this was antithetical to the art of storytelling. The sanitizing forced on Hollywood's writers by the House Un-American Activities Committee represented a radical departure from tradition.

Something precious was being smashed under McCarthy's ideological hammer, and it was getting replaced by formulaic, plot-driven writing. **Two-dimensional characters, symbols rather than representations, were pushed plot point to plot point.** After a few entertaining and, hopefully, nail-biting twists and turns, came a final confrontation and climax, after which the protagonists arrived where the audience had expected them to arrive. This was a destination as wholesome as it was bland.

The new party line was that in the USA, society had been perfected and had reached the apex. The view was of a nation that was quite literally God's country, and so it was up to the individual in God's country to sort out his or her place in it. Only after finding their place would he or she be fulfilled. If there is a threat to that fulfillment, it stems from a personal flaw, or it is because of an alien threat.

This is not as it always had been. At the time of the establishment of this nation, the leading figures of the Enlightenment on both sides of the Atlantic believed in reason and science. Their supposition was that all faiths needed to be examined for what is reasonable in them and separated from what is the product of wishful thinking or superstition. As Benjamin Franklin put it, questioning authority was the duty of every citizen of a free nation. This core idea defines modernism.

The role of the individual in society – as reactionaries like McCarthy would have it -- was quite the opposite of what Franklin had in mind. It was more consistent with the 8th century than the 18th, which was when the United Stated was conceived along with it with its startling aspirational addition to its Constitution and the Bill Of Rights.

And so it was in the late Forties and early Fifties that revisionist rules for storytelling were introduced. These were formulaic rather than an open-ended process based on free will. These tales were meant to reinforce the common consensus rather than to challenge it. The "self" in these formulas is uncovered rather than forged in front of the audience in Act Two. **Essentially, there is no inner journey in the revisionist view, just the outer one.**

These vapid caricatures were symbols of an ideal good –or the opposite, symbolic of the bad. The social order here is as natural and as perfect as it is stilted. Each protagonist finds his or her place in this frozen cosmology and accepts it with gratitude (which is "good") or rejects it out of ingratitude (which is "bad"). In this universe, fat girls only find genuine happiness in the arms of fat boys. Because, from acceptance of your place comes happiness.

The good news is that everyone has a place in the "natural hierarchy": janitors are meant to be janitors, bosses are meant to be bosses, soldiers are meant to be soldiers, slaves are meant to be slaves, housewives are meant to be housewives, fat girls are meant to fall in love with fat boys, and, of course, cops are cops.

A common formula features a humble protagonist who does not "believe in himself" but in Act II learns to believe in himself and when he does, he levitates to the top of the heap, defeats the bad guy, and is crowned top-dog. Act III has him clasping the hand of the most beautiful and perfect female in the land, before his adoring subjects. He is just a little shy, just a little bewildered, and humble. This show of humility is in the job description of "hero" and, now buttressed by the love of his princess, he stands square-jawed, muscular, and beaming before the cheering multitudes who beam right back at him. Now all is right in the land again. It is back to neat and tidy, and the only threat to the Disneyesque happy kingdom is from an alien threat.

You have seen that movie. You have seen it over and over again, and when it is done right you've enjoyed the ride, like you've enjoyed the amusement rides in

theme parks like Disneyland. But where did you travel to?

This kind of storytelling is a mechanical fill-in-the-blanks exercise, in which empty vessel protagonists and antagonists are ranked by the story in a way consistent with the conventional understanding. The conventional understanding, however, is not left to evolve. It is handed down to the beaming masses. Hollywood, of the mechanistic new age, is viewed as having a special responsibility in that engineering project.

It does not take much of a stretch to imagine that people with a social engineering bent would be drawn to a method of telling a story similar to an engineering project. This is one of the changes out of the dark anti-democratic era that emerged in the USA after World War II, and to a considerable degree, Hollywood has remained tamed.

It is not that there were no formulas for writing fiction before the Fifties. There were many hack writers in the studio days filling in templates, and some were skilled and gifted. They worked fast to churn out scripts for most of the "B" movies of the era, but the formulas then were mostly scaffolding. The storyteller still had to invest the main characters with an interior life, and there was that old game-changer, free will, at the epicenter. This emphasis on free will decision making was, in fact, emblematic of the best American storytellers, perhaps because the USA was the first child of the Enlightenment.

7. From Art Imitating Life, To Life Imitating Art

The communist boogieman provided a convenient excuse for attacking "subversives." Who is a "subversive" depends, of course, on who is doing the attacking. HUAC conflated the term with critics. They had a broad interpretation of "subversive" and "commie." But an economic collapse, sandwiched between two catastrophic world wars, left a lot of people questioning premises.

And it is true: Nowhere, not in factories, coal mines, or even in universities, did "subversives" have more sway than on the movie screen, or in the new flickering box in living rooms.

I am not referring to the few overtly, politically left movies like The Salt of the Earth or The Grapes of Wrath. I speak of the garden-variety Western or noir flicks of the era. With few exceptions, their anti-hero private eyes, or cowboy heroes, were maladjusted outsiders. If they were dwellers in the gritty city, typically they were broke, borderline alcoholics, and at the end of their collective ropes. Wholesome, they were not. Company men, they were not. Joiners, they were not. Lonely, they often were. Happy, they were only sometimes. Free, though, they always were, except not from their moral obligations. They were chained to that.

In the movies of classical Hollywood, these outsider heroes were pitted against not just a corrupt social order, but an entirely corrupt society in which most people support a kind of tyranny favoring sociopaths. (An exception is Capra's great Christmas film, It's a Wonderful Life. Jimmy Stewart's protagonist, George Bailey, who it seems is about to be punished for his fundamental decency, is as surprised and delighted as the audience is when the people he had helped through the years rise up to support him.) These are heroes who do not march to battle leading the broad masses. They fight, normally alone, against the odds, using their individual smarts, individual fists, and individual guns. They are individualists to the core. A key difference between these movies, and what was to become the new boilerplate, was that, often as not, the bully was not only in a position of wealth and power; he was emblematic of a social class.

It should not be a surprise that depicting the threat against well-being as coming from the "top" was unacceptable to the "top." The "top" preferred a threat that came from outside savages who whooped and hollered as they rained flaming arrows on courageous European settlers.

No doubt, a great many American writers at the time understood that, and when they buckled under to HUAC, they betrayed something greater than just the storytellers who refused to kowtow to the McCarthy gang. It is not a coincidence that these real American citizens were like the fictional citizens of the town in High Noon who abandon their sheriff. The sheriff is left alone to confront a gang of villains who, the story makes clear, represent corruption. Carl Foreman, the writer of High Noon, really had been a communist, but had left the party years before. He was, nevertheless, blacklisted because he refused to give names to HUAC. Everyone in the Hollywood system, by then, knew the score. Most also knew that buckling under to HUAC meant departing from the mission statement for storytellers.

It was not just ego that caused the "winners" of the American competitive game to want Hollywood to cast them as the (perhaps, thinly disguised) heroes. This was viewed as necessary to social stability. A threat to the status quo and the common consensus was easy enough to prove, since it was built into the American Constitution, and some people followed it. This threat was not just one perceived by members of the Chamber of Commerce. It was felt by millions of Americans as a threat against the "good." For these citizens, the social hierarchy was not just inherently "good," it was preordained by God. They were, therefore, "good" because they supported the "good." It was circular logic sealed in a bell jar, but dad gummit, they were gonna stick with it.

It had not escaped the notice of these "good folks" that many writers and directors in Hollywood had not been born in the USA or were children of Jewish, Russian, Italian, Catholic, German, and God knows what else. These "immigrants" were perceived as an alien threat.

To these racist, reactionary "good folk," the problem was as plain as the nose on Jimmy Durante's face: a foreign element had imported foreign ideas into the USA. After the Second World War, these "good folk" seized the day.

And so, it happened. A freckly blond jazz singer who, like Jazz itself, was not known for being an especially "decent" girl, got the Hollywood whitewash. Doris Day became the epitome of the corn-fed, ample-bosomed young ladies whose charms were clearly visible but who would offer them up only upon the altar of marriage. Her charms were a weapon. Her prime tactic was the sexual tease. On screen, "Mr. Right," who would pop the question after enough sexual frustration, was someone like Rock Hudson.

8. Writing A Script From A Script

Nonfiction goes after the facts. Fiction hunts out the truth. But they work in tandem. In Hollywood, storytellers had been free to hunt truth –if it made money. It had. Boatloads of money was generated off the clattering typewriters of leftists like Dashiell Hammett and Raymond Chandler. Politics had played small, even in their tales, as it did for those in Hollywood who got to keep their jobs. In old Hollywood, job security was dependent on the good ol' American bottom-line.

The starting point for storytelling, then, even for mediocre movies –even if the storytellers themselves were not always conscious of it– was neither an idea nor an ideology but life as it is, regardless of the genre. The ending point was, and is, what brings value to life. That eclipses politics.

Noir protagonists could barely stagger out of bed in the morning. Outwardly, there was little to distinguish them from the common garden-variety loser. Inwardly, there was that moral compass pointing to where, often, even they did not want to go. The fight to do what was right was lonely. Taking it on was as likely to make enemies as friends. Taking it on, though, was irresistible –even though, God knows, these protagonists usually tried to resist. It is hard to argue that, by extension, there was not a sense of disappointment in the USA underlying at least some of these movies, and certainly in some of the best.

This attitude was subversive, however, only to the extent that such tales subverted complacency and undermined gullibility. It should go without saying that people like Ben Franklin, Thomas Jefferson, and Tom Payne would be delighted by such storytelling. (This should go without saying, but clearly it needs to be not only said, but proclaimed into the ears of many present-day script writers.)

Even if there was often more shadow than light in the America depicted by Hollywood between the wars, it was just storytelling reverberating with history and the 20th century reality. This was art imitating life, not life imitating art. The American mainstream adored these films precisely because the hero refused to take a dive. That struck home and pay-dirt.

There were, to balance the ledger, movies that idealized the leisure classes and starred suave actors such as Fred Astaire, Carole Lombard, or William Powell. They portrayed the pampered gentry living in a society where each had a place. Class conflict was minimal. Audiences also enjoyed these flights of fantasy in which ladies wore designer gowns to lunch, and men sported top hats. People did not deny reality, however; they just enjoyed a vacation from it.

A less fanciful reality was depicted in other movies, but equally appreciated. Importantly, in any of these films, even if the gangsters, representing corruption and bully power, emerged out of brutal social conditions, it did not excuse their crimes. There was no glorification of violence in noir films.

In the 1931 movie, Public Enemy Number One, the gangster, Tom Powers (James Cagney) knowing that he is about to die at the hands of the "dirty coppers" begs his mother to forgive him. The skeletal old lady is living in dreary deprivation, her body broken by brutal hard work and grinding poverty. This is how life is, bleak, the movie is implying. Yet, Ma Powers' sense of right and wrong remains heroically noble: she refuses to acknowledge this gangster as her son.

Fast forward a few years, and the private eye outsider becomes the insider cop, an often charmless, puritanical martinet. Bad guys by the late Fifties tend to be bad to the bone, emerging not out of social conditions, but out of primal evil. Characters now discover their fate, more than make their fate. This is how drama becomes melodrama and writing becomes mapped out, engineered as if from a schematic. Good guys wear white hats; bad guys, black. Good girls do not –not until they are married. Married people sleep in twin beds. The head of the Ranchers Association, the villain in the suit who, in the previous era, robbed honest hardworking farmers either with a pen or a shot in the back, morphs into a wise, wealthy, generous patriarch on a ranch called the Ponderosa. Ben Cartwright is the father we wish we had. The TV series Bonanza was a well-crafted, reassuring, hierarchy-affirming Western melodrama with much of life's nuance gone. Each episode was like a teacher's lesson plan, with every lesson assuring us that God is in his heaven and things are the way they are because they are meant to be that way, and have to be that way.

This revisionist storytelling was centered in a cosmology frozen in stasis, with each person locked into a social order that should not be fundamentally questioned, never mind challenged. That was not, in itself, new. In fact it was old, very old. It had been that way in Western civilization for centuries, from the fall of Rome until the thaw known as the Renaissance. With that came the emergence of modern science, followed by the European Enlightenment and the development of ideals upon which the USA was established. Now we were supposed to go back to that?

When storytelling is not on the scent of the elusive truth, the storyteller is not doing the job.

There were many poor movies made before the purge, and plenty of good movies made after; but something had shifted in Hollywood. Movies like High Noon or TV's The Phil Silvers Show, made within the shadow of HUAC, had been skeptical about the social order. Then quite suddenly, writers and directors of these kinds of movies and TV shows found themselves swimming against a very strong current. It had not been like that when benign neglect had been the rule in the studio system. As long as the film was profitable, the bosses did not care.

The term that emerges after World War II is "commercial entertainment." "Commercial entertainment" was American and good; everything else was labeled anything from "artistic" to "serious" to "European" and foreign. The idea embedded in "commercial entertainment" is that this is American Entertainment based on the kind of storytelling and filmmaking that caters to the audience's tastes and interests. "We serve the people" was their motto –or their excuse– for doing this. Everything else delivers themes and messages that mainstream audiences simply are not interested in – and should not be. Of course, no proof was offered, just the general contention that you really should not ask too many questions.

This "everything else" was written off as impractical, even arrogant; as if in other places –foreign places–

storyellers and moviemakers set, as one of their main goals, to NOT make money.

Ludicrous as this idea was, most Americans bought it off the rack, and most Americans have remained convinced that there is a kind of storytelling from other places that appeals only to oddballs, sex fiends, "eggheads," and foreigners. Foreign, in this context, did not just mean people from other nations. Foreign, in this sense, meant "un-American." There were many writers in America deemed un-American.

I refer to the coarse, commonplace, and wrong-headed notion that entertainment precludes any serious examination of what matters in life. You, as a storyteller, either do either one or the other. You either entertain or you do this other, foreign thing –and "ordinary people" are simply not interested in foreign anything. Ordinary people, call them plain folk, demand entertainment. They are not all that smart, they aren't particularly interested in smart, and smart isn't all that important anyway. Smart can be suspect, as inferred by that tawdry phrase "too smart for his own good."

Many people either forget, or do not know, and do not want to know, that between the wars, fabulously successful films by directors like Howard Hawkes, fired machinegun dialog laden with innuendo, puns, nuances, and sly political references, at a broad audience of farmers, doctors, housewives, soldiers, hardware salesmen, and university professors alike – that is, ordinary people – and ordinary people got it and loved it. These scripts were rich with ironies, jokes, observations, social criticism and insight, and the contemporary audience was right there laughing, applauding, getting it all without effort. This is not just a tribute to the writers and directors of the time, but equally to their audiences.

And so it was that the art of making movies, as a journey to meaning, became quite suddenly suspect in the Land of the Brave and the Home of the Free. Writers and filmmakers who created fantasies to shine light on reality were on the way out. Those who wished to replace reality with fantasy were on the way in.

It is also true that American movies have always tended towards escapism, but before Joe McCarthy, the escape had meant a vacation from the grey, dull, daily grind. After McCarthy, the escape meant from the truth, and maybe even the challenges of the soul. The agrarian vision of Jefferson, with its romantic ideals born out of the European Enlightenment, seems to have manifested a nation of salesmen and engineers. Moviemaking, like that loathsome, formulaic, five paragraph, fill-in-the-blank essay writing methodology foisted on American school children after World War II, was broken down into components, systemized, prepackaged in books and manuals, and sold to new generations of storytellers and filmmakers. Just to be part of the "entertainment business" was now quite enough.

The new methodology, whether intended or not, catered to those who wanted to avoid thinking too deeply in a brave new era when thinking deeply was suspect. It catered to audiences like that, and storytellers like that. It was to them that the torch had been passed. **The quest for meaning was set aside in favor of a quest for pleasure, status, riches, romance, marriage, and other aspects of "normality." Normality was where you were supposed to find meaning.**

41

Instead of unvarnished insight into the human condition, instead of shining a flashlight into smoke and shadow, writers would plug in a chain of tropes that were symbols of or pointers to something inferred, something that everybody, supposedly, somehow knew. If you were cool –that is, if you were extremely cool- the parade of memes and symbols was exhilarating and meaningful. Period.

Because we knew what it was all pointing to, didn't we? If we were American we knew. Real American equates with real cool, end of story. Who does not want to be American? Putting up a hood just before the protagonist does something dangerous or bad, or shooting a gun sideways, was, and is, hard-ass American, whatever that was –and anyway, it was enough to carry a story to the next plot point. The audience kinda,sorta knew what this was all about, the way the subjects of some ancient, imaginary emperor knew that he wore the most beautiful clothes.

Something organic had been remade into something ersatz and mechanistic. For a great many people today, storytelling that can be separated into components, assembled, packaged, or repackaged, and sold as commodities, is how to do the job in Hollywood. It is enough. And it might also be sometimes entertaining, but it's the wrong job.

We also know this: The best movies, plays, and novels do not follow that model –because they cannot.

The problem with many of the books on storytelling and screenplay writing available today is they treat stories as commodities. They should not. They should be treated as art, as a particularly practical and universal sort of art. To concentrate on the craft, at the expense of the art, guarantees poor art. You need both.

This book about storytelling, I hope, is different. It is theme driven, rather than meme driven. It too is based on a methodology, not invented, but simply passed along. It is fair to say that it is obsessed with life's big questions. It further contends that this is what audiences and readers, beginning with very young children, want and need from a story. We are the animals who want to know, not just how, but why. Whether audiences and readerships are aware of why they want to be told a story is not terribly important. You, however, you who wishes to master storytelling –it is important that you know.

PART II

THE STORY OF THE STORY

1. Story Theme

Keep asking yourself, as you craft your tale: what is my point here? What truth, or truths, will I be getting at? As a storyteller, this is your decision to make. Make it, and make it early.

You will need to establish the foundation for the theme in Act I. The audience, or readers, do not have to "get it" –and maybe should not "get it – until the climax of Act II. But you, the storyteller, must "get it." Throughout the process of telling the tale, you must keep asking yourself; how do my main characters' actions and words promote what I am trying to get at in the whole of this tale? It is not enough to be witty or clever. How do the decisions of my characters result in the actions of Act II? How does that move the plot forward to that penultimate moment of truth, the climax? How does the entirety illuminate the theme? For it must.

And you must make "theme-driven storytelling" your practice. It is the key to everything else, including the storytelling mechanics. All stories are driven by themes, which are universal truths for all humans. For this reason, the best tales easily travel far and wide.

One way or another, we all face these truths, and how we face these truths is our personal story. Storytelling is the art of shedding light on truth. This is done not by argument, but by example. If you do not have that truth in your mind (firstly) and embedded in the set-up in Act I (secondly), then all that follows will fail.

You must do the work to discover what your tale is about, or you will never be able to tell it. So, what is it about? What is it you want to get at? Why should the audience or readers care?

The theme of Shakespeare's Macbeth has to do with ambition. Unbridled ambition calls down the forces of hell upon Macbeth, and everyone he cares about. Hell does not come on them willy-nilly; it is not Fate visited upon them, but the direct result of Macbeth's choices, which are acts of will.

In Act I, ambition is triggered in a heroic man through the agency of three witches, who tell him that he will become king. It is a prediction. They are just giving the Scottish lord a wee push. Shakespeare takes pains to make that clear. All the cackling witches know through magic is this otherwise noble man's great weakness. They also know that Macbeth has no legitimate claim to the crown, and so he will only realize the prediction if he decides on treachery. The wicked witches put this into motion. That is all. Their evil magical powers are limited to that push. Now it is up to Macbeth.

This is important: The witches do not cause Macbeth's downfall. Macbeth does. Having chosen his path, he makes his fate. Macbeth, like all well-written protagonists, has free will, and no one, no magic, not even witches, can take that away from him.

For Shakespeare, making a moral choice is everything. The outcome of that choice is secondary. Sometimes the protagonists die as a consequence of making the right moral choice, as do Romeo and Juliet. Making the right choice does not mean that you get the happy ending. There is, after all, wickedness in the world as well as outside agencies which are beyond the mortal coil.

The overriding theme of all Shakespeare's histories, comedies, and tragedies has to do with the relationship between free will and fate. Does fate make you choose what you do, or do your decisions make your fate? Is character fate, or fate character? Not just for Shakespeare's protagonist but for all protagonists, in all good tales. The moral choices remain theirs –witches or no witches, antagonists or no antagonists. **The onus is on the protagonist. Without that, the most you have is a parade of events leading to an outcome, which is not a story.**

The theme of Little *Red Riding Hood* is that if you are too naive for this world, you are in danger of being devoured by wolves. In most cases, this would be a wolf in disguise. Sometimes this is a wolf in sheep's clothing; sometimes he is decked out in a short-sleeved white shirt and an ugly tie and sells cars; and sometimes the wolf slicks back his hair and takes you on a date. In Little Red's case, the antagonist is a wolf ludicrously dressed as her Granny.

Mom tells Little Red in Act I that she wants her to deliver a food basket to Granny. It is a big responsibility. Is she ready to take it on? Is she adult enough yet? Thus, the theme is embedded.

This story is intended for small children. The theme relates to what is important to them, as all themes

49

must for their intended audiences. What is important is that our children grow up to be responsible adults. They will need to grow up, alas. The little kids in the target demographic intuit what drives the tale, even if they can't articulate it as a theme.

An audience, unlike a storyteller, does not need to articulate the theme. (Unless they are English literature majors.) But the theme does need to strike home with them. If Act I is properly set up, the audience will understand that this is about taking on adult responsibilities. They will get it, even if they could not quite say it. They already know from personal experience that kids like them naturally want to grow up, and also kids like them naturally want to play pretend. They want to grow up, and they do not want to grow up. It is a dilemma that the best of us never quite solve. In any event, they will identify with young Miss Riding Hood.

Unfortunately, Little Red Riding Hood is a tragedy in the Shakespearian sense. The youngsters learn that growing up requires being aware that there are wolves that connive to eat you in the woods. It is an awful truth, and, in this case, as in all fairytales, the theme is also the moral of the story.

Not all themes are morals, but all stories hinge on protagonists choosing a course of action. They are forced to make choices in situations created by antagonists. When Little Red enters Granny's cottage, she sees what is plainly a wolf ludicrously dressed as her Granny. She could have chosen to run. Had she the "right stuff" she would have assessed the situation in a nanosecond and high-tailed it out of there.

Red may not know, but all the small children in the audience know, that this plainly is not Granny. Instead of doing the obvious and fleeing, inexplicably the gullible little twit chooses to step forward and ask the wolf three incredibly stupid questions. This is pure foolishness. All the kids know that as well. They know that they would not have made the same decision, and so they are not entirely terrorized by this turn in the tale. They are little children, after all, and it would not do to scare the bejesus out of the wee mites ... or would it?

The onus is on Little Red to make the right decisions. Antagonists can only force the protagonists to make a choice. **Without the exercise of free will, there would be no "hero's journey" and no illumination of themes. For stories must not just communicate a basic truth about life, they must illuminate these truths.**

There is a type of storytelling that aims to teach a lesson, and by no means are all of them directed at children. The Bible is a series of moral tales, some better than others. In fact, this kind of storytelling represents the bulk of both testaments. And so it is that the moral of Little Red Riding Hood is beautifully echoed in the King James Bible: "When I was a child, I spoke as a child, I understood as a child, I thought as a child: but when I became a man, I put away childish things."

The Bible is a collection of stories because storytelling is how humans sort out what is beneficial in life from what is detrimental. The same can be said of the Bhagavad Gita, the Quran, and all wisdom literature. All successful stories meet this requirement, even if most are not the lessons that end with the venerable phrase, "And they lived happily ever after."

Theme is the engine of storytelling, but not just any theme will do. Only great and abiding truths about life can serve this purpose.

There can be more than one theme driving a story, but they need to be related. Facing the loss of his possessions, his children, and his own health, Job refuses to curse God. This theme relates to choosing the greater good over the personal good. After all, sacrifice is required of the true hero. That can include sacrificing a marriage, losing your friends, or giving up the respect and adoration of society –all for the greater good. **Nobody said being a hero is easy, and no hero should have it easy. Put them through the mill.** (Batman: The Dark Knight, High Noon, and a great many other fine films and novels are driven by this kind of theme.)

2. Know Your Audience

Before you start writing, you need to know who your target audience is to be. Twilight, a very successful series of books and movies, targets the interests of pre-pubescent and teenage females. The characterizations and plots of this series are compelling for many, perhaps even the majority, of females within that limited demographic. Fifty-year-old males do not fall within Twilight's demographics, but neither do fifty-year-old females. Commercially, this is not a major consideration. This swathe of the general audience is deep enough for these stories to do very well.

On the other hand, Little *Red Riding Hood* tends to be captivating if you are four to perhaps eight years old. Roughly by age twelve, audience buy-in begins to fall drastically. So, if the eighteen and older set is your target demographic, this particular story needs to be rewritten as horror, parody, or satire; and has been written this way many times, often successfully.

I will restate it this way: Your story theme must matter to your target audience. If that target demographic (demo) is broad, your theme must be compelling to that broad segment. It is more difficult to cater to a broad audience than a specific one, and a broad but shallow demo is not necessarily superior to a smaller but deeper demo; and not just in terms of money-making.

3. Outlining The Rules For The Three Act Structure

There needs to be a three-act structure for any tale. Aristotle called the three acts the Beginning, Middle, and End. And he was a genius, so who are we to argue? In any event, this is the Aristotelian sense of "Act" used throughout this book. Can you remember beginning, middle, and end? Good. Now, when someone informs you that a certain story has, say, six acts, please explain to that person that they are subdividing.

Really, it is difficult to imagine a successful story without that basic, Beginning, Middle and End, three-act structure. Yet, in my experience, more than a few beginning writers manage to do just that. They might believe they have three acts, but do not. They might believe they have more than the three acts, but, if the story is working, they do not. It could be a case of having different definitions and that might be just a semantic difference, which might not be terribly important. **What is important, however, is to understand that each act of your story has a different function and that if the beginning does not satisfy, then neither will the rest of it.**

This is what matters:

1. Act I needs to introduce what the story is about, meaning the theme, or themes.

2. Act II is comprised of tests and challenges meted out to the protagonist that illuminate the story theme.

3. Act III supplies an ending that satisfies the story theme established in Act I, and the action in Act II.

The kinds of errors that result from ignoring or not understanding the above are common, even in produced movies. After watching a film, if you get that familiar feeling that you have been led up the primrose path, only to leave feeling somehow dissatisfied it may be because there was no foundation or theme in the tale. Or, if there was a theme established in Act I, it did not relate to the action in Act II. Or, the summation in Act III did not satisfy, because it bore no relationship to what happened in Act II. In all these cases, the audience has been cheated. The storytelling has failed.

4. Each Act Has A Different Function

Not only do you need to fashion a Beginning, Middle and End for your tale; you must accomplish certain goals specific to each act. For example, for the story to come to meaningful life, it is critical to convey the story theme(s) in Act I before proceeding to Act II. If not, your tale is already rolling down the tracks towards a burnt-out bridge.

We will explore this in more detail later, but from the start, make sure of the following:

1. In Act I, the audience needs to know what is at stake, and who is involved with those stakes. What is at stake is built upon the foundation of the story theme you establish in Act I. Act II will contain most of the action, but all the action has to be about what is at stake. If it is not, the action, or, if you prefer, "what happens," will be off the story spine. (More about that later.)

2. Act II is where the story happens, but what happens is dependent on choices the characters make. Those choices are driven by the story theme introduced in Act I. If the theme has not been embedded in Act I, in Act II the story will fall apart, no matter how exciting the action might be.

The theme is illuminated through character development. This is how the audience eventually finds out whether or not the protagonist is a hero. Does he or she have the character mettle to achieve what is at stake? Is what is at stake worthy of a hero?

Remember, the story is dependent not on whether the protagonist becomes the hero or not. It is dependent on whether the storyteller succeeds in illuminating the story theme, and getting at meaning. If the story conveys that, regardless of whether it is comedy, tragedy, Western, fantasy, murder mystery, thriller, horror, action adventure –or any genre– the story will succeed with its intended audience.

Act III is triggered after the second act has reached its climax, which is the penultimate, make-or-break moment of any story. **Act III ties it up with a bow. Every Act III needs to bring the story to a satisfying, if sometimes**

temporary, conclusion. There is nothing wrong with an Act III that hints at a sequel, but that is a secondary, and not a "must do" function.

5. A Limited Yet Almost Infinite Array Of Choices

Although a storyteller has infinite choices for how to tell his or her story, there is an even greater infinity of ways how not to tell the story. **There are limitations to what engages and satisfies an audience, and there are rules of the road to obey on the hero's journey.**

There were many earlier versions of Romeo and Juliet before Shakespeare did it right. You've never heard of them, have you?

PART III

THE THREE ACTS

1. Constructing Your Three Act Structure

An act consists of at least one scene. A scene is one event. There is no theoretical limit to the number of scenes in an Act, as long as they further or deepen the story. A scene can occur at one location, or it could be a contiguous event and move through many locations, such as a car chase.

a. Act I

Act I introduces the story theme, although not necessarily by explicitly stating it. **The theme acts as the locomotive that pulls the train for the hero's (the protagonist's) journey.** For Little Red Riding Hood, the story theme might be stated as, "If you are too naive for the woods, you are in mortal danger of being devoured by wolves."

Act I reveals Who, When, Where, and What Seems To Be The Situation. Act I introduces at least one protagonist and at least one antagonist. An antagonist can be a force, such as a hurricane. But usually it is a character.

Taking Little Red Riding Hood as an example:

WHO: Little Red is the protagonist. "Who" is also the Wolf, the antagonist. He puts Little Red into danger. Like all antagonists, his job is to test the protagonist (in this case, Little Red.)

Mom is a secondary "who." She sets out the theme by giving the goodie basket to her daughter, instructing her where to take it, and explaining that this is a job for a "big girl," someone who will not dilly-dally, someone who will not play on the way.

Mom would be considered a supporting role. Granny is in the same category, and is only mentioned in Act I. Granny does appear, albeit briefly, in Act II. Her role may not be as significant as the role of Mom. Her job is to demonstrate how an adult reacts when she sees a wolf.

WHEN: For Little Red Riding Hood the "when" would be: Once upon a time, in the agrarian and bucolic past.

WHERE: This refers to the primary setting, the starting-off point for the journey. For Little Red Riding Hood, we know it is somewhere in Europe, near or in a forest. (The story was written in France.) Act I, Scene I is usually set in Little Red's family home. Act I, Scene II is set in the woods. In your own telling of this tale, you might choose to have an establishing scene of the small town in the woods as well, and perhaps other supporting scenes; but in any version, you need to have the scene when Mom gives Red the basket of goodies, and gives Red her marching orders.

WHAT SEEMS TO BE THE SITUATION: The situation is as follows: Granny is not feeling so well. Mom asks Little Red to go to Granny's cottage in the woods and deliver her a basket of goodies to eat.

Little Red agrees to take on the responsibility, but does she understand that this is serious? How serious? Is she up to the challenge?

To restate, the story theme of Little Red Riding Hood is know the woods, know what lurks in the woods, and know how to deal with it –or perish. The theme is not directly stated, but the next scene has Little Red skipping along with her basket on a path through the woods, and not looking particularly concerned. There she meets a Wolf.

Like all worthy antagonists, the Wolf switches the story onto different tracks. The situation has now been changed, and we enter the challenging territory of Act II.

b. Act II

Where Most of What Happens Happens

Act II is the meat of the story. What happens in Act II are tests. Act II consists of one or more tests of the protagonist's character mettle. The tests are based on the story theme. In a successful Act II, you get insight into WHY the story turned out the way it turned out. It is not enough to just convey what happened and the results. There needs to be revelation.

Most commonly, Act II depicts a series of tests, not just one. Each test lasts at least one scene. It is the protagonist who is tested and, through those trials and tribulations, the story theme is revealed. In a movie, revelation is achieved mainly through the action, and the action mainly takes place in Act II.

Words are not actions. In Act II, things need to happen, not just be said—or maybe not even said at all– but conveyed through dramatic action. Shoot-outs are one form of action. A trial can be action in a court-room drama. There are as many options as you can imagine. But a movie is not a play: action drives the story more than words do. For a movie, it's "show it" over just "say it."

Storytelling is a process of controlled revelation. It is not an essay, which is an exercise employing logic and facts to prove a point. In a story, the process of getting at the truth is placed within a human skin and sent on a human journey. The audience is human, after all. All stories, in this sense, are road stories.

Luckily, there is no need to reveal the complete truth; that seems to be beyond us anyway. Fuzzy and incomplete truth is good enough for us humans, and good enough for that conglomerate called an audience. Light, though, needs to be shed. Light must be shed on aspects of what is important on the human journey. The best tales illuminate quite a lot about that little matter of what is important and what simply is not. This is what the controlled revelation reveals.

In practical terms for the storyteller, however, revelation is the aggregate result of choices the protagonist makes in Act II. The protagonist, one way or another, is forced to confront these choices, which are foisted upon him or her by the antagonist. The choices always involve virtues. Will the protagonist choose the path of virtue, or some other path, such as the path of expedience?

It is the audience's appreciation of why a protagonist fails or succeeds that makes a story a success or a failure. The audience needs to appreciate why. A story finally succeeds or fails at the climax of Act II. **A proper climax**

answers the "why" question. This is when the protagonist finally wins or loses, slays the dragon or is slain by the dragon –and there is an endless variety of dragons worth slaying. It is all about virtues such as honesty, courage, kindness, generosity, and sacrifice –that sort of thing. But it is not enough to point that out; the real question is, why choose virtue at all?

"Why," in this sense, can be thought of as the third dimension of storytelling. It makes a product of the imagination seem real. Without satisfying the "why," a story will fall flat. It is not important how much is blown up, how many heads are lopped off, or how much sex is depicted. A lot of sex, or a lot of violence, will neither make nor break a tale.

RULE OF THUMB: You need in your Act II as much sex, violence, controversy, thrills, let downs, uplifting moments, and twists and turns as it takes to get at your story theme. No more, and no less, than that.

In every Act II, choices are forced upon the protagonist, in the form of obstacles placed in the path on the hero's journey. Commonly, just when it seems the way forward is clear, it turns out to be a trap. Little Red should have seen that it is not her granny in bed; it is a wolf. She does not. The audience does. The little kids, the target demographic, certainly get it. It is clear to them by the climactic moment that Little Red does not have "the right stuff." The little mites understand what the "right stuff" is, in general terms at least. They have been guided to that understanding. They understand that a clever little girl would know that this is a wolf, and a wolf is a wolf, which is the point of this particular tale. In all cases, by the end of Act II, why this particular "right stuff" is the "right stuff" must be crystal clear to the audience.

Exactly how to shed light on the story theme embedded in Act I is up to the writer. But the result of that creative labor has to be clarity. For the audience of Little Red Riding Hood, clarity can be stated as "The consequences of being too naive for the woods can be dire." It does not matter that children are not likely to be able to express the theme verbally. Little Red lacks "woods smarts," and we all live in some sort of woods or another, which is why this tale appeals almost universally to little kiddies everywhere. They get it.

Light has been generated in this little tale through the friction of the protagonist versus antagonist dynamic. This is always what generates the light. This process or revelation, of clarification, occurs in every Act II of every successful story, from Dostoevsky's Crime and Punishment to the next Batman thriller. Friction needs to be there. Tension needs to be there. Conflict of some kind is absolutely necessary. **If the friction is right, the fiction will be right**, and Illumination of the story theme will result –abracadabra. Like a magician who has practiced her tricks, to the audience it looks easy; but really, she has the right stuff after not having the right stuff for a long while. She had to practice.

About this "right stuff," it is not any "right stuff." It is "the right stuff," which is matched to "the right theme." As you write Act II, constantly ask yourself what qualities of my protagonists are being tested, and how those tests will reveal your theme. You are trying to land a slippery fish. First you need the right bait, and then you'll need the skills, which is another term for "the right stuff." It is not always easy, but you will net that slippery fish if you have "the right stuff." So choose your tests in Act II for the right reason, because they will lead to the revelation of your story theme or themes.

If you shoot a script as a movie, all tests in Act II that do not shed light on your story theme, no matter how exciting, well-choreographed, deftly shot, or masterfully directed, will end up on what was once called, the "cutting-room floor." A good editor will do the same to your novel. The best time to prevent this painful and often expensive mistake is in the writing phase. The best way to limit the meandering away from your theme in your writing is to know your theme beforehand. What are you trying to get at? What is your point?

Remember: The tests given to the protagonist by the antagonist should escalate in peril. Each test should bring us closer to that decisive moment at the end of Act II, the story climax.

In Act II, protagonist and antagonist need to be good dancing partners. They need to be well matched, so the outcome is uncertain until the climax. You can fool the audience on the way so they feel that they know the outcome, but do that only to tease them. Rip the floor out from under them soon after. Uncertainty keeps the audience engaged in the story.

Throughout Act II, keep your audience off balance. If they feel that they have regained their balance, knock them to the ground. Wham!

Never forget why you are employing your antagonist. This is to test the mettle of the protagonist. These are not any old tests, but the right tests, based upon the theme you set into motion in Act I. Each test in Act II has to be based on the story theme. We call this sticking to the story spine.

With few exceptions, after each test, or as a consequence of each test, something else needs to happen that raises the odds even more against the protagonist. With almost each escalating plot point, your reader or audience needs to be thinking that a successful outcome is even more unlikely.

The feeling you are after, as storyteller, is that disaster lurks just around the corner. This is the case whether your tale is light romantic comedy or a war story heavy on the violence. In all genres, a hero who succeeds must succeed against mounting odds. After all, the purpose of all storytelling is not just to test the protagonist, but to test the story premise –meaning its theme. Does this theme really hold water, or are we fooling ourselves? Maybe wolves really do not want to eat naive little girls. Maybe it was just bad luck that Little Red is devoured. My guess is that the author of this fairytale would disagree with that premise.

The climax of Little Red Riding Hood occurs when Little Red is pounced upon and suffers a, burp, belch, horrible, painful, yucky death -- which sometimes happens, even to cute little girls. If that was all there was to it, however, there would not be a story –just maybe a news report under the headline, "Small Girl Eaten By Wolf." The point is that according to this tale, if Little Red was a more woods-wise and attentive young lady, she could have avoided her fate. The point is also, therefore, about the nature of fate.

Please note: The climax of Little Red Riding Hood delivers on the theme laid out in Act I. It does not deliver on any old theme. You must do the same. Chain every plot point, not just the climax, to the story theme.

A plot point, for example, wherein an antagonist lures a protagonist into a dark alley, shoots him, and leaves him for dead, might be brimming with excitement and peril, but will add nothing but confusion to an Act II that, let's say in this example, should be testing the trust and fidelity of a love relationship instead; unless the bit of business links back to the relationship in question. This would have to be a relationship set up in Act I. Everything that happens in a tale after Act I needs to have its seeds in Act I. If you can link your exciting, peril-laden bit of storytelling business to your set-up, keep it. If not, discard it. By "link" I mean, connect it to your story theme. Your story theme is what-it-is-all-about. So, what is it all about?

If you understand what your tale is about and can think of a better way to get at what-it-is-about, choose that way, and discard the weaker plot point in favor of the stronger. Harden yourself and learn to be ruthless about what stays and what goes. Make it your ironclad rule: **No matter how well written, intriguing, or exciting an Act II plot point might be, if it does not do its job, it needs to go.**

Ask yourself what you are trying to get at here. Each plot point in Act II has a particular job. If two plot points do the same job, fire one. Again, this is dependent on you knowing what your tale is about. The earlier you realize what the job is, the better. **The earlier you get rid of elements of your story spine that are not doing the job, the less rewriting you will have to do.**

c. Some Variations On A Theme in Act II

Let's take an example where the story theme –"what it's all about"– is trust and fidelity between lovers. Maybe it is a husband and wife. Let's say this is, as the old blues song puts it, "that hound dog of mine gotta quit doggin' around" tale. It could just as easily be a "You do not miss your water until your well runs dry" tale. More prosaically, this is a tale told to reveal the value of fidelity, the reason why lovers should remain true to each other. Of course, maybe they should not, but that would be for a different tale. The teller of this imaginary story, however, vehemently holds that fidelity is a virtue and cheating is a vice. The act of cheating on your sweetie constitutes a betrayal. Let's just lay this one out that way. This, then, will be our Act I departure point.

There may be good reasons for that point of view, but the storyteller's job is not to preach as much as to prove, not for a court of law, but to an audience or readers. **Proof, in a story context, is demonstrated not through argument but by depiction.** Furthermore, the theme needs to be wrapped in human skin, and the leading human –the protagonist– needs to be set on a journey wherein events befall him or her that test both the protagonist and the theme. The antagonist is the creator of those events.

What is depicted in Act II also has to connect to life as the audience experiences it. The audience does not have to have been in a war to connect to what happens to the characters who are literally in a war. The setting, war, can be metaphoric, such as a divorce war. **What matters is that whatever happens in your war story must connect to some kind of war that the members of the audience are intimately familiar with.**

Secondly, the audience must not only identify with your protagonist. Your protagonist must appeal to them. "Appeal" in this sense means "identify with,"

regardless of whether or not the audience approves of the conduct.

The audience must care about the fate of the protagonist. They need to be on the protagonist's side. They need to be put under a spell through your storytelling magic so that they care. It is the kind of magic that can be learned, but not so easily mastered. What's hard to master is not the mechanical aspects of casting spells, but the wisdom behind casting each and every one of them –in other words, being a wizard, someone who has insight, someone wise.

You need to wise up fast because the audience needs to be on the protagonist's side no later than by the end of Act I. Act I is where audience buy-in happens. Entering the territory of Act II without this buy-in portends disaster.

Audience buy-in simply means that the audience is now hoping for a positive outcome for the protagonist. Throughout the course of Act II, the storyteller should be dangling this hope in front of them –and then maybe snatching it away.

Ask yourself, "Why should the audience care?" "How do I make them care?" Let us not mince words about this: the audience has to be made to not just care about the protagonist but to want the protagonist to achieve hero status. Whether that happens or not by the end of Act II, however, is not relevant to the success of the tale. Some protagonists become heroes at the climax; others do not. What is important to understand is that the storyteller needs to maintain control of the emotions of readers and audiences throughout the bumpy journey of Act II. If the storyteller gains control of the audience or readers, it will not matter if the protagonist ends up as a hero.

It does not matter to the success of a tale if the protagonist fails to slay the dragon, but the fate of the protagonist has to matter to the audience. Learn to make that distinction.

What matters is that the audience has been hoping for a positive outcome. If that does not happen, they should be left in distress, grief even. If it does happen, they should be elated. Either way, if they care they will be well satisfied with the show.

Do not have any qualms about being a merciless manipulator. Manipulate the crap out of readers and audiences. By opening the book, or sitting down in the theatre, the audience has agreed to allow you access to their minds. They want you to wave your magic wand, and open the portal to the land of fiction where their disbelief is suspended. The audience wants to be in that state and anticipates the moment when they are transported to storyland. They will enter the land of fiction naturally and effortlessly, if you know the magic.

As far as the outcome of your tale, it only matters that the audience understands why the goal was attained or not attained. The protagonist, or protagonists, as the case may be, do not have to live "happily ever after." But if they do, they damn well better have earned that Hollywood Ending.

How should be in service to *why*.

All that happens in Act II, all the trials and tribulations foisted on all protagonists by all antagonists, also known as the plot, needs to be driven by the theme. Theme is the engine of plot. If a theme is not embedded in your tale by the end of Act I, the plot will be re-plotted and replotted again, and whatever the outcome, your Act III, the conclusion, will not satisfy.

Getting back to our exemplary story about fidelity, or perhaps the lack thereof: The protagonist in our imaginary Act II could be trying to remain faithful to his one-and-only in our "you ain't nothing but a hound dog" tale. Maybe he will succeed, maybe he will not. As indicated previously, that is not instrumental to the success of the storytelling. Plots are meant to be played with. Themes, not so much. **Themes are the Big Issues of life.**

Now that we know what our Big Issue is –what our theme is– the plot will be crafted to test for the virtue of "fidelity." That is, the pressing question becomes, "Why should our protagonist remain faithful?" Maybe he should not have to remain faithful. Here is where we must shed light. We can now narrow down the Big Issue here to: "What, if anything, does being faithful accomplish?" Maybe it is just a social convention, and when circumstances change, maybe the rules of the game can change as well. Or maybe not. Shall we find out?

Given this rejiggered theme, the storyteller could, as one out of thousands of possible devices, choose to add the significant other's best friend into the mix. This new character will now take on the role of an antagonist. She or he can lure the protagonist into a dark alley in an attempt, in this case, not to shoot, but to seduce.

After all, shooting the protagonist might take the story somewhere we do not want it to go. It might take us off theme. That depends, but for the moment, let us say that lovemaking serves the story better. Audiences tend to have a taste for the lurid, so, by all means, throw in sex –especially if it is a more effective "bit of business" to get at your given theme than murder and mayhem would be.

Every Big Issue gives rise to Big Questions posed in Act II. This particular event, or scene, properly managed, is guaranteed to give rise to Big Questions, and the audience will expect answers. Will the protagonist be able to resist this vixen or not is not the Big Question. How strong is his moral fiber and why this is important, is. Can he tame his inner hound dog is not the Big Question. Should he, is. What is at stake? His marriage, assuming we have established his marriage?

To put it another way: does a few moments of illicit pleasure necessarily have to be an inhibitor to long-term happiness and wellbeing? What is at stake? When do you sacrifice happiness for pleasure? Is this ever right? Is this a betrayal? Is betrayal ever right? What are the consequences if the protagonist succumbs or, alternatively, does not succumb?

Consequences in a story cannot be arbitrary. Consequences are subject to poetic storytelling logic that is based on the theme, the "what's this about" that you have established in Act I. **You set out the rules for the journey In Act I, and then the journey begins in Act II.**

What subsequently happens, and the consequences of what happens to the protagonist, must make sense to the audience. That necessarily means that what happens, no matter how fanciful, needs to somehow dovetail with the life experiences of your target demographic. That will occur only if your theme is meaningful to the intended audience. Otherwise, your entire story will end up meaningless to your audience. You need to be audience obsessed. It does not matter if your tale is meaningful to you. If you have failed to illuminate an aspect of what has lasting value in life, as your audience experiences it, you have failed.

Knowing to whom you are directing this tale is vital. For our imaginary story, the target demo will be adults. This will not be the audience for Little Red Riding Hood. These are people who have reached puberty. They have faced, or might face, a similar situation. They know this territory. They are in a position to judge if what you are portraying rings true.

So let's say you have created scenes that test the mettle of our protagonist's character and stick firmly to the story spine. So far so good. **Now the challenge is to keep them on the hook. The tests meted out to the protagonist by the antagonist, your best girl's best friend, have to relate directly to your theme –fidelity– and what happens subsequently has to remain on the story spine**. The consequences of passing or failing those tests have to matter within the poetic logic of your story, and must matter to your audience as well. So do not fail them.

Now let's dig deeper. There is a lot more on your "to-do" list.

This theme of our imaginary tale –"fidelity"– can be further refined to "betrayal." Betrayal is an aspect of the greater theme, but betrayal is more specific. **The more specific your theme is, the more powerful the web you spin out from this theme is likely to be.** This genre might be romance, but any genre only serves as a stage for the Big Issues. This Big Issue involves honor, loyalty, and, most of all, not hurting those who you claim to love and cherish.

But life is not simple, why should stories be simple? So what if, either way, your protagonist will lose something he values? What if you cast your protagonist into circumstances where he is cut off from hearth and home?

He is cut off from what he has valued and is experiencing an understandable human need for intimacy, some relationship that is life-affirming, some hope to bring him out of despondency, and perhaps to offer him meaning again.

Or what if he meets some stranger on this journey who needs that from him? What if they are both decent, well-intentioned human beings cast into dire circumstances such as war?

Dire circumstances offer endless opportunities to investigate meaning, do they not? Let's say there is another protagonist, and she is beautiful. And they are both beautiful and they are both desperate for hope and happiness, and then, et voila, hope and happiness present themselves. What if?

So many "what ifs," How do you sort them out? On the other side of the ledger, what is the Big Issue about betrayal anyway? Why love? Do people really ever love, or is this only a tale we tell ourselves? Why is it bad to sexually betray someone, anyone? What is the big deal? Why does it matter? If they will not know back home, where is the harm?

Anyway, what do you get out of "staying true?" What is the payout, if any? A new experience is being offered. What do you gain by turning your back on it? Maybe you should not. In fact, if pleasure knocks on your door, why not just let it in? You live for only so long. It is all up for grabs, at least it should seem so in the tale well told.

Remember, we had established that the Big Issue for our imaginary sojourn is betrayal of those whom, supposedly, the protagonist holds dearest. Thus, our hound dog with the wandering eye can succumb when the opportune moment presents itself and our sexpot, now back to being an antagonist, exclaims, "Oh poop! I broke my heel!"

That is up to the storyteller since what happens is up to the storyteller. What is not up to the storyteller is that this must be a free will choice, foisted upon the protagonist by an antagonist but made by the protagonist. It needs to be a choice, and there have to be at least two courses of action. **No choice equals no test, no furthering of a theme, and no light shining on the meaning of life. No illumination on that little matter equates to no story worth telling.**

d. Free Will

Storytelling absolutely requires the exercise of the agency of free will. Why a given protagonist chooses one action over another makes it a story and not just a parade of related events. The job of the antagonist is to force choices on the protagonist. The choices, such as to betray your true love with someone else, become actions, and all actions have consequences. Again, these choices that lead to actions that, in turn, lead to consequences, cannot be any old choices, actions, or consequences. They all must be on the story spine; which means, they must advance the plot towards the revelation of the theme, which happens at the climax.

It is always, at bottom, a moral choice. It is always, at bottom, a test of the virtue or moral fiber of a would-be hero. Some protagonists prove their mettle and end up heroes; others fail the test. Whether or not the protagonist slays the dragon and wins the hand of the princess is not what makes it a tale well told. That is a "what." "Why" is where any story lives or dies. "Why" is what a story seeks to reveal. "Why" is meaning and meaning lends value to life. **A story has to shed light on the meaning of life. Nothing short of that will do.**

As you craft your Act II, keep asking yourself what choice is being foisted on your hero, and how that choice furthers the revelation of theme that comes at the penultimate point of any tale –the climax at the end of Act II.

So back to, "Oh poop, I've broken my heel!" The protagonist can now either carry the antagonist in his arms, out of the dark alley and into the light where he can play the gentleman and fix her shoe. Alternatively, he can decide to stay in the dark and succumb to her "lips of honey" as the Bible puts it in a similar story concerning King David.

A protagonist can rise above his inner hound dog, or not. King David did not. This Big Issue, there as here, has the animal in us pitted against our higher angels. This is a fertile ground to cultivate for writers, just as the Nile Valley was for the agrarian civilization of ancient Egypt –which is where many of the tales in the Old Testament originate.

Remember, though, when writing fiction, you are not writing a Miss Manners manual or, God forbid, a spiritual guide. Which wins out, animal or angel, is not a central concern of fiction. That is just a plot element.

You had better have, however, at least a dollop of insight into your Big Issue. Do you? If not, tell a story about what you do have insight into. The cliché is, "Write what you know," but I find that this is too vague. Often this is taken to mean, for example, do not write about war unless you have been to war. That is what in the American parlance is called "hogwash." What is key is providing insight, not literally sharing the experience. It matters not what you write about if you can pull that rabbit out of your hat.

The good news is, you do not need to know everything before you start writing. If it happens, that is great, but a storyteller, like many a protagonist, can stagger into the light.

Maybe you will need a dozen rewrites. You would not be the first. Every storyteller has his or her unique creative process. That is okay, as long as you keep in mind throughout your creative process that insight into the story themes is what you are after. Beethoven also struggled. Mozart, not so much. The music is what mattered. The story is what matters. Who can say who is the greater composer or writer?

It absolutely does matter that a story theme is skillfully embedded in every Act I. It absolutely does matter that every Act II is a proving ground for those universal theme(s) embedded in Act I.

In Act II, things are made to happen by you, the storyteller, usually through your antagonist. Reacting to what happens; the protagonist takes action which changes the course of the tale. In turn, the antagonist reacts to those changes in a way that ups the risk to the protagonist. This goes on until the end of Act II. This is the meat of your tale. This is how a storyteller sheds light on a universal theme. You are not an essayist. You are not debating. You are showing.

Theme is the engine of all storytelling. No engine and you cannot take your audience or readers anywhere. You can go back to Act I and fiddle with or hone your

77

theme, but each change to the theme, even in nuance, will change what happens in Act II. This means what happens in Act II will happen differently. The sooner you clarify what your tale is about, the easier the writing tends to go.

Bearing that in mind, let us tweak our love story example's story theme again, and not just a nudge: This tale is now about seizing true love firmly in your hands even at the risk of that hurting others. For what hero does not take risks? Betrayal now takes a backseat to this new theme: **Happiness. Happiness at what cost?**

Happiness is not just a Big Issue; it is the mother of all Big Issues. Every story is about that. How to attain happiness is a human dilemma for which there is no definite or entirely satisfactory answer. This is convenient for storytelling. For it does seem, almost by design, that in every life, "damned if you do, damned if you do not" knocks on the door more often than does"true love."

We are now deep within storytelling territory, but this time the theme is not satisfied by a simple moral. This leaves Little Red Riding Hood in the dust.

With this revised theme, a villain can be again hired to lure the hero into a dark alley, shoot him, and leave him for dead. Why should he? Because he is a villain. Because all villains are agents of the storyteller helping the author propel the plot towards the climax. That is why, in this version, the protagonist will be nursed back to health by an angelic damsel. They will fall in love and, at some inevitable point, they will do what comes naturally to lovers. But, of course, there will still be the wife left behind.

And here we go. Damned if you do, damned if you do not. It is an interminable dilemma: can you go through life without hurting the people you care about most? Possibly not. This way, though, a plot point that had not served the theme in earlier versions –a shooting– is now on the story spine. Now that the theme has been altered this way, you can pay off this plot point. The audience will love it, drawn as they are by the allure of sex and violence. (Please stay tuned: we will return to this unfolding tale later …)

Every plot point needs to pay off in terms of its story theme(s), if a tale is to hold sway over its audience and propel Act II to the climax. This is what I meant when I suggested that a good storyteller is a wizard who has mastered the art of controlled revelation.

As a member of the audience, though, despite the twists, clever turns, and switchbacks of any given plot, there can be little doubt that the audience has seen movies or read novels based on this theme many times before.

There are only so many themes, and most writers are aware of this fact. You have also come across most plot points before. And so has the audience. Yet you, and I, and the audience, will eagerly suspend disbelief and read another book, or watch another movie, or show, based on rehashed themes and plots that we are familiar with. We cannot get enough of "good tales, well told." If a tale impacts our lives, if it sheds light on our personal struggles and the dilemmas we face, you and I and the audience will fall in love all over again. All stories that are well told rise out of the flames reborn, like the mythic phoenix.

What particular tales resonate with you is an individual matter. Different stories suit different folks. Some themes speak to some people but not so much to others. A professional writes with her audience or readership in mind. As with wine and food, a tale goes better when properly twinned with an audience.

Act II is where the story theme comes alive through the characters and what happens to them. Character arcs are married to story themes. Story themes all point to what really matters in life and to what really does not. **Every Act II presents the protagonist with at least one dilemma that must correspond to the theme and, simultaneously, must tie into what is faced by the readers or audience on their life journey.**

Death is probably the mother of all human dilemmas. Happiness is probably the only effective weapon we have against death. E**very story, in one way or another, pits happiness against death.** The protagonist's job is to pursue happiness of one kind or another. The antagonist's job is to pursue death of one kind or another. It could be literal death, or figurative death, such as the death of a marriage, or the death of honor.

e. Act III

Act III sums up the tale. Act III pays off not so much Act II, as Act I. "All's well that ends well," claimed Shakespeare, but he also knew that what ends well in Act III needed to be set up well in Act I.

By the end of Act II, in The Godfather, the audience already knows the answer to the question, why the youngest son of Don Corleone, a Mafia don, ends up as violent and corrupt as his father. This occurs despite the son's heroic efforts to break away from the family business. The audience has seen it happen plot point by plot point. They have seen life break young, idealistic Michael Corleone. More importantly, since the theme is how corruption robs the soul, they suspect that they would break too in similar circumstances, and so they sympathize with him, and understand his fall from grace, even as they are revolted by his violence.

The climax of this particular movie depicts not the zenith point of a hero's journey, but its nadir. This is how it goes when writing tragedy. By the end of Act II, Michael Corleone has been devoured by his dragon. Since the audience already knows this and since it's an iron-clad rule of storytelling that every scene needs to add something different and something more, **Act III cannot simply repeat what we already know, or recap it. The function of Act III is to point back to Act I.**

Not being able to end your movie properly is a common problem, but the reasons why are not commonly understood. **If you find yourself writing an unsatisfying Act III no matter how many times you rework it, it may help to go back to Act I** and rediscover what it was that you were trying to get at from the beginning. If there is no theme stated or implied there, you are in big trouble. You may have to re-write or abandon the project. Let it be a learning experience, and you will not have wasted your time. **Write to theme. Stay on the story spine.**

Even if you think you have your theme, you might have to clarify it for yourself, and that means for the audience as well. Then, you need to make sure that what happens in Act II adds up to a revelation of that exact story theme. You may have to remove some plot points, add others, and perhaps play with character traits. It would be a partial rewrite. But it can succeed because now you know why certain elements need to be crafted one way and not another. Now you have a rubric to guide your storytelling decision making.

It usually comes down to a failure to have internalized one key concept: The job of storytelling is to reveal something about the meaning of life.

In Act I, you state a premise. In Act II you test that premise through your characters. You create, in this way, a **character arc**. At the climax at the end of your second act, the protagonist manages to win or lose, or something in-between. **In Act III, you delineate the results of what happened after your protagonist passes or fails the tests.**

You had been testing the methodology of your protagonist in Act II, and the audience had been paying attention. The audience wanted to know if that methodology would make "Jack" a hero. You kept them wondering, and that kept their attention. Most beginning writers understand this part of the storytelling process but, for the storyteller, whether a given Jack manages to slay a given dragon is not what's most important. Meaning has to be revealed through Jack's journey to the story climax. If a little of the meaning of life had not been revealed, you, the writer, would have failed to slay your own dragon. This would be the writer's journey as opposed to the "hero's journey." You too will need to slay your dragon for your tale to succeed. Your Jack bears no such burden. Jack goes down gloriously to defeat. That can work, as can the hero going down ingloriously. **These are plot points.** Important as plot points are, they need to serve a greater purpose. The storyteller who has failed to miss the distinction between theme and plot will tend to have problems tying her tale up in Act III. It is not impossible that there is nothing to tie up. If the storyteller has neither identified the theme nor embedded it in Act I, rejiggering Act III will be a waste of time.

Too many how-to-write-fiction books emphasize plot and character development, but fail to emphasize that they are two parts of one whole; and that whole is a success only to the extent that it sheds light on the human journey. Real humans tend to be neither entirely heroic nor thoroughly villainous, and that might also be true of your main characters, but real humans necessarily will always be deeper and more complex and contradictory than characters in a story.

Ask yourself this: Just how did your Jack earn the princess, or fail to? Did the dragon slaying methodology employed by your protagonists –be they male, female, old, young, handsome, beautiful, average, ugly, human, a cartoon human, human in the guise of a duck or a rabbit– wrestle with virtues such as honesty, humility, courage, kindness, patience, diligence, loyalty, generosity, to name but a few. Was that portrayed? Because this must be what is at core, albeit portrayed through characters, since storytelling, especially in Act II, is always about virtues versus vices. The protagonist can win this wrestling match, or lose; but the test of character mettle defines Act II. Even every Superman story is about that. Each episode's Act II re-tests the "Man of Steel." Act III of each episode merely ties it up with a bow.

The point is *why*. Why, or why not, do they do the right thing? The storyteller must provide the reasons through the plot. A dead hero or a dead dragon is merely the outcome of the plot. A plot is not a story, and some dragons prevail no matter how virtuous the hero. That

83

greatest of dragons, Death, kills every Jack eventually. How Jack lived, though, is where your story lives, or dies.

Perhaps your Act II demonstrates that courage alone is not enough to slay a dragon. A hero also has to be resourceful to slay a dragon. By definition, a dragon is stronger than any human and good at its job. (If the dragon is not good at its job, slaying it has no value.) To win this fight, a human has to use his noodle because his human noodle is his only true advantage. If your hero fails to use his or her noodle, as in the case of the Little Red Riding Hood, the dragon gets its lunch.

The original Act III of Little Red Riding Hood fittingly ended that way: she was just eaten. Years later, well-meaning adults overly worried about traumatizing little kiddies added a hunter who cuts out Little Red from the wolf's stomach. This is a pity. These well-meaning adults were no friends of the storyteller. That Act III is weaker than the original. Using your noodle is sound advice when faced with a more powerful adversary, and little kids who fail to learn that lesson may also end up as someone's lunch. Do not pull your storytelling punches. Give your tale an Act III it has earned. Be wary of "political correctness."

The fictionalized hero's journey inherent in every tale steps in for our real-life-journey. Despite the suspension of disbelief, the audience is aware that the story only depicts fictional heroes and fictional dragons. **The trick is to connect your fictionalized dragons with what your target demographic tends to contend with in their real lives and to their real need to slay them –or maybe, to make peace with them. That will guarantee their buy-in and attention. Then, having depicted something about the worth of the battle against**

those dragons, your Act III should just about write itself.

2. The Situation My Situation Is In

Giving advice is not always the storyteller's job. **A story meant to advise is just one type of tale ending with a simple moral, such as in the case of *Little Red Riding Hood*.** The classic 70s movie, The Godfather, has no simple moral. But it has an initial situation in Act I which, when it changes, leads to an Act II, as it does in Little Red Riding Hood. Both stories succeed, and a large part of the reason why is that the audience buys into the situations. But why should they? Why does an audience accept a storyteller's fictional situations? This is not so simple. **If you are hoping that the audience will automatically suspend their own reality and accept yours, forget it. You need to earn their buy-in.**

When you tell a story, you are creating a fictional reality, with fictional situations. Whether your audience accepts your fictional situations or reject them hinges on whether they ring true to them. Are the fictional situations in your tale pertinent to the target demographic of your tale? Your audience need not have directly experienced a situation, such as an actual battle in a war, as long as they have battled something or someone. A mean mother-in-law can fill in for almost any dragon.

No doubt, in their real lives, the people in your target demographic are up against competitors who want what they have; or they, themselves, might want what others have. All resources are limited, but some resources are more limited (and more critical for you) than others. Life

85

itself is a limited resource, but in a time of war or disaster, it becomes important. Liberty can be a limited resource. Finding the right spouse usually pits you against competition. The resources people are interested in will vary, but the urge to be selfish and just take will always be pitted against the higher angels of our nature.

Life might not always be a "hardscrabble," but every life seems to have a certain amount of "hardscrabble" built into it. That is not always a bad thing. Life being easy when you are young can actually cause "hardscrabble" when you are older. Lives that are too easy can make for meaningless and boring lives. And boring too can be a "hardscrabble." That is called irony. It is impossible to get around the irony that the "hardscrabble" in life can be the ticket to what is valuable and gives meaning. Every story is concerned with revealing exactly that. When I suggest that conflict is essential in every good story, this is the reason why.

There is the exterior "hardscrabble" and the interior "hardscrabble." Everyone engages in these battles, consciously or not. **The situations in your story need to echo situations common to your target audience or readers.**

The members of the audience want to project themselves into your story. Your protagonists need to be their avatars. **The audience is guaranteed to project themselves into your tale if you portray the battle of virtue and vice that rages within themselves.** They are eager to do so as long as the situations in your tale resonate with what they deal with in their own lives. Give them the opportunity to sort out what is important and meaningful in their own lives. Write from that perspective. Give them situations they can relate to.

Situations where someone wants something, but loses the chance because it turns out that he or she did not deserve it, are common enough. If your plot begins with a boy whose girlfriend gives him the boot for some rather good reasons, that would be your opening situation. Winning her back, then, could be what is at stake in Act II. The decision to win her back changes the situation, and that kicks off Act II.

Remember for whom you write. Also, remember it might be called "storytelling," but you are not just telling. You are depicting, in this instance, how a lad might or might not triumph over his base, self-centered instincts and access his higher angels. Only then will he finally deserve "true love" and win his princess. It is not all that important though if he does or does not win the princess from the perspective of the storytelling. **Do not confuse plot with the point of the story.**

Whether the protagonist does or does not gain back his girlfriend is only another plot point. All sorts of things can befall a protagonist. Perhaps said princess finds "true love" with someone else, and our hero is left out in the cold. Or maybe he is the one who finds "true love" with someone else, and she is left out in the cold. Both are what we call plot points and represent plausible situations with which to end Act III. How that final situation is derived is where you need to concentrate most of your efforts.

You are depicting a process that challenges one or more main characters in ways pertaining to a story theme. All situations your characters face should be calculated using that metric. Whether your protagonist succeeds or fails to achieve the goal set out in Act I – whether he slays or is slain by his or her particular dragon– and how that affects and changes a protagonist is called a **character arc**. The character starts one way and ends another.

The situation established in Act I has to be radically altered by the antagonist. The train had been going in one direction, which seemed to be the situation. But the situation has changed and now the train is chugging into unchartered territory. Now the story is becoming interesting.

Act II is where most of what happens happens. The tests of character mettle in Act II provide most of the "action" in any tale. These tests are meted out to the protagonist by the antagonist in your name, dear storyteller. The antagonist is your agent. **Or you might even think of it this way: The antagonist is you, and the protagonist is your audience.**

The purpose of the tests is to illuminate the theme of the story through character development. Thus, the theme is wrapped in human skin. Thus, a story is not an essay. Thus, through storytelling, what is important in life is smelted out of what is not important. What is important in life equates with what is meaningful in life.

You need to keep the audience guessing about the outcome. That is how you create suspense. By keeping the final situation of your hero's journey uncertain, you hold the audience in a state of suspense and, simultaneously, in a state of suspended disbelief. You keep them under your spell. You compel them through your stealth, your craft, and your guile to discover what will happen next.

A good storyteller is a dirty sneak who toys with his or her audience, and who plays with their emotions

fairly ruthlessly. Depict that twisty, bumpy, perilous road towards enlightenment and happiness viscerally, give the audience protagonists they care about, and they will be right there with you to the end of Act II, otherwise known as the climax.

But when they pass through the climax and pull into the terminal station known as Act III, they will expect a pay-off, which may or may not be "and they lived happily ever after." No matter. **They will not regret the journey you put them through either way, if each bump and twist and turn finally makes sense.** Act III is a summation. It needs to add up. It needs to add up to insight into the audience's own lives. **Insight is the pay-off for all stories well told.**

The pressing question is: what makes the wrestling between your baser impulses and your higher angels valuable and meaningful? Why does it matter? Or does it matter at all? **Of course, as storytellers our answer has to be yes, it matters. But more critically, it needs to matter to your target demographic. That is why they laid down the price for the train ticket. It does not matter if they know that or not. You have to know that. This is the craft you are forever learning.**

La Romance

We were talking earlier about depicting a boy-girl situation. I suggested that the more of a dilemma a love affair is, the more the audience will be interested. Most people seem to relish little more than a good gossip about other people's romantic dilemmas. Why? Can it be that this particular human situation digs right down to the happiness question? How does loving someone who loves you

89

back make you happy, and what happens if it does not? There is your meat.

Clearly, the romantic relationship is the box, but what matters is its content. Sex is not a relationship. Mammals coupling is not a relationship. Sex can be the glue of the box, but is never the meaning. Pleasure is pleasure. There is nothing wrong with it, but if your target audience does not already know that pleasure does not equate to happiness, it is the wrong target audience. It is the content of the box that matters to the lovers as it does to us busybodies. We had been talking about a boy-girl story. What is at stake in a romance? Is it the relationship that is at stake? Who cares about that but the people involved? What is compelling for the audience is how a romantic relationship provides transportation to what is meaningful in life.

Clearly, the relationship is the form, but what matters is the content. Sex is not the relationship. Mammals coupling is not a relationship. Sex can be the glue of a romantic relationship, true, but never the meaning. Pleasure is not happiness. A romantic story is about both form and content; but ultimately it is the content of the box rather than the box itself that matters to the lovers, and so it is what also matters to the audience.

In terms of this kind of hero's journey, a romantic journey, what happens along the way is definitely more important than the destination. Two lovers were physically attracted to each other, coupled, and made a baby. Eventually they died, knowing that their babies had made babies. What is new, and so what?

To cast your genes into the future might be the "biological imperative" but it is not intrinsically meaningful to us. How can life be the purpose of life? If that were a satisfying answer, there would be no romance genre. The Holy Grail for every romance tale is, again, to shed light on what is truly meaningful on the human journey. Of course, this equally applies to all storytelling genres.

The content of all successful romantic tales is what the sexual relationship does for those "in love," in terms of the delivery of not just sexual pleasure but happiness. After all, you do not need a partner to achieve orgasm, do you? If all we are after is bodily pleasure, why would we even seek out a relationship? The answer every romantic story provides to that question is that sexual pleasure is a means to an end. Or at least that it should be. Every successful romantic story sheds light on why that is. Why is intimacy conducive to human happiness for most people?

Lovers either grow internally within a sexual relationship, or they do not. They cannot quite pull it off, or they manage to. They grow together, and stay together, or they grow apart, and part. ***Why* is what really matters. The lovers serve as surrogates for the audience. All protagonists are surrogates for the audience. Why they stay together or why they separate is what matters to the audience. They already pretty much know everything else about this situation. Sex is not much of a mystery, but this is.** Why are two sometimes better than one at the happiness game? Why is pleasure not the same as happiness? Whatever the genre, the job is not to disclose how, but to shed light on why.

This kind of theme, then, would be about the nature of the self, the purpose of intimacy, and the transcending of self we call unselfishness. Romantic love implies caring for someone more than you care about yourself. From a romantic point of view, humans need this. That points to

91

the "why." This "why" would foment both the beginning situation and final situation. By the end of Act II, it could go either way. The act of letting go is just as compelling as the act of coming together. What is in it for them, either way, is the question. This is what the audience has a pressing need to find out. Certainly for most of us, finding a soulmate features prominently in life's to-do list.

What matters in a story equates to what matters on the journey of every human life. Act I, for this reason, ends in a situation that can be described as a predicament. The audience buys a ticket for the ride to find out how that predicament works out. They care because they are faced with similar predicaments, but the predicaments they are facing may not be as apparent as the ones in a story. Usually they are not, which is another reason why storytelling is an essential cultural component for all human societies.

Humans are sentient beings who need clarification. Stories serve that purpose. Or they should. Make sure yours does. Make sure every situation you create serves to move the story towards clarity. Your purpose is to shed light on the overall situation we call "a life."

Every Act I begins with a situation which is threatened or destroyed by an antagonist. The protagonist(s) now faces a different situation, one in which suppositions are challenged throughout Act II.

We are born. We try some things. We succeed at some, fail at others. We engage in various sorts of battles, some outer, some inner, most both –and we win some battles and lose others. The final situation we all find ourselves in is the one where we lose the battle. We all know that, but, perhaps, on the way to our final battle, we might find someone and make a baby. Perhaps we manage to raise some children. Then comes the day we die. Then our children do the same. And so on ...

Who are we to believe that any of this matters? In a universe of billions of stars and billions upon billions of planets, Earth is a speck of dust. Earth is lost in all this vastness. Who do we think we are? Why not just take as much as we can and give back as little as we can? Why is it important that we earn something rather than get it for free? (The comic romance film Arthur is built on this theme.)

Happiness seems so attainable for a dog. What does a dog know that we do not? What do we know that a dog does not? Why are we unlike the other animals?

This defines the human situation all of our situations are in, and the Big Questions that are our universal themes. Our situation provides raw ore for storytelling. A storyteller mines, refines, smelts, and creates something meaningful and, I would go so far as to suggest, useful from the raw ore that is the universal human situation.

For those who seek perfection, storytelling might not be your field of endeavor. Life remains a mystery, and storytelling has been described as "an attempt to articulate the unutterable." That is quite a trick. You need to be quite the magician. The situation is messy. The logic of the storyteller is fuzzy. You need to practice your act but, even so, all your successes are doomed to be some degree of failures. No story entirely succeeds. Every word, at some level, betrays the truth. We mortal story smiths are nevertheless compelled to try to get at the truth. It seems that the need to shed light is integral to the human condition. We must at least try to articulate what is important about life. This is our mission, but we are not alone. Amateurs do it too. They do it at the bus stop. They do it when they gossip around the water cooler. They do it by telling a joke. Sports talk is but a metaphor for the meaning of life. We storytellers are, however, the professionals. We must learn to do it better.

The following needs to be said upon bended knee: Mystery is the situation we all find ourselves in. Meaning has to be coaxed out of mystery's shadow by artful magic. What a storyteller decides upon as the starting situation of a story is governed by what particular aspect of the mystery he or she is arrogant enough to attempt to illuminate. If that sounds metaphysical; if the storyteller now seems cousin to the shaman or priest; so be it. Just do not let it go to your head.

Here are some down-to-earth rules:

1. The starting situation reflects the story theme. As with any situation, ask yourself, where am I going with this? Make it a habit. The starting situation must change to advance the audience, in tandem with the hero, toward a final situation. No side trips allowed. (Best advice: If you can, know where you want to go before you start going.)

2. A starting situation never lasts. The change, a trick accomplished through the agency of an antagonist, propels the tale into Act II.

3. Act II exists because there must be a quest for there to be a story. Ultimately, the quest is for meaning that must be earned to be learned. In Act II, one situation becomes another when an antagonist forces a protagonist to choose a course of action. The result is a new situation that is also the result of what the protagonist had chosen to do.

4. Antagonist and protagonist act as partners for change, which might or might not be positive. That protagonist and antagonist are dancing partners is not always so apparent but remember, when the Highway Man says, "Your money or your life," he offers a choice. The onus is always passed on to the protagonist no matter the circumstances.

5. The situation "without" changes in tandem with the situation "within." This inner situation consists of emotions, psychology and even philosophy, and it is more critical than the outer. Both must be present.

6. More books and films fail, not because the plot was weak, but because the storyteller did not understand how characters change internally as plot progresses, or he or she was not able to communicate this. **How and why a protagonist changes must be conveyed to the audience.**

7. The outer is servant to the inner. **There must be overall protagonist growth, or the opposite, through Act II.** Remember, some of the best tales end tragically.

8. Inner journeys correspond with outer journeys, yet need not end the same. It is the inner journey that is primary. A hero can be slain by a dragon. The final scene of Act II can be hero as a pile of cinders. Yet he or she can die undefeated, inferring success on the inner journey. In this case the protagonist dies nobly which implies an extraordinarily virtuous person. Only if noble status is earned does a protagonist succeed in becoming a hero. The hero's journey must be understood as a perilous climb up the mountain to slay some dragon, but what makes for a hero is not if he or she reaches to top to kill the dragon; rather, it is defined by whether or not he or she triumphs over their inner dragons.

9. Any "born hero" is a boring hero. Heroism must be proven and earned.

10. The hero can perish in the effort of slaying whatever dragon links to the story theme, and **the story will either succeed or fail depending on the quality of the quest and the quality of the protagonist, not how the quest ends.**

11. Protagonists endure escalating tests of their character throughout Act II. They go from dire situations to even more dire ones. How they tackle each test is what promotes them to grow `inwardly and to succeed or not. (Hamlet and Macbeth are both failed heroes.)

12. Act III depicts the aggregate consequence of those trials on the protagonist during the endurance course of Act II. **Act III is the final situation in which "They lived happily ever after" –or they did not.**

3. Plot

1. The starting situation in Act I is based on the story theme(s).

2. The starting situation needs to be, at least, somewhat familiar to your audience, because they have to project themselves into it. This is true whether the story is set 5000 years in the past or 5000 years in the future. This is true regardless of the genre of your tale.

3. The initial situation needs to change. The premise set in Act I needs to be challenged. The floor must fall out from under the protagonist.

4. When the initial situation changes, it will be through the machinations of one or more antagonists.

5. The new situation confronting the protagonist(s) will be less familiar and more perilous—for we are now in Act II, Scene I.

6. Act II is where what happens, happens. The situation keeps changing –and escalating in risk– because the action is directed against the protagonist by the antagonist.

7. The job of any antagonist is to test the character mettle of a protagonist. That process is what sheds light on the story theme.

8. All of the above, and all storytelling rules, are fuzzy and are governed by a story's internal logic, which is also fuzzy. This is art, not science.

9. Master the internal logic, however, and you will master the plot.

Rote learners be warned: Just memorizing rules or following a chart will not make you a good storyteller. There is internal logic to the craft that needs to be understood and acquired. From that understanding, the utility of the rules listed above will become apparent. **This will provide you with a framework for how events unfold in a tale –i.e. how they must change, where they are going, and why. Events are set up in Act I. Events unfold in Act II, which is where what happens, happens. What happens is also known as the story-plot.**

You will need to work within the confines of the internal logic of a story, but there is no reason to feel trapped. Hopefully it is obvious to you at this point that you can't write just anything. The reason is that you are working toward a goal, and it would be silly to think that just anything will get you there. Some things can happen in Act II and some things cannot. Nevertheless, there remains an almost infinite array of possibilities for how to get your story to where it needs to go.

There is no use engaging in the storytelling exercise if you leave your audience disinterested, or scratching their heads. **You do not want to just get your protagonist to the climax at the end of Act II. You want the audience to accompany the protagonist on her journey. You want their sense of self to evaporate as they subsume the role of story protagonist. The protagonist must serve as their surrogate.**

This means that effectively you, as storyteller, have two masters. Bow down to them both. One is internal, powered by the beating heart of your theme. The other is external, powered by your audience and their compelling interests. You do not necessarily need to pander to their sensitivities or be afraid of threatening their beliefs. Threatening their beliefs is part of the job. The good news is that the audience actually wants you to threaten their beliefs because it serves to clarify their beliefs and to deepen their appreciation and understanding of life. This is actually why they lay down their money. But do not tell them that. Let them believe that all they want is to be "entertained."

If your tale merely serves to reaffirm what the audience thinks they already know, you are not doing your job. Your plot has to take the audience somewhere else. If they arrive in Act III where they started, you have taken your audience nowhere. You have cheated them of insight. You have shed no light. You have served a false master.

You only need to keep the audience under your spell from Act I until Act III. That is all. That is the trick. Fortunately, maintaining their buy-in also has its own built-in logic.

For storytelling, the key is in the "what's-it-about." Everything goes back to that. Everything is driven by that. "That" is the story theme. You need to understand your theme and then that understanding will guide the exploration of that theme which is Act II –where what happens, happens. Act II can be thought of as the journey of the protagonist(s) to the center of the theme. The theme is always an articulation of what makes life worth living. Once you get a grip on that, Act II will be where you play with it, turn it inside-out, put it on its head, or send it ass-over-backward. **That will be your plot.**

That stated, your time would be better spent pondering your theme than pondering your plot. Once you have internalized what your story is about (theme) the events that add up to your plot should fall into place relatively organically and with less effort. This is not to say that coming up with a plot is as easy as falling off a log, but it is something that can be accomplished considerably easier once you get a grip on the theme. Just keep in mind that this is not about mimicking a formula. This requires insight.

If you are unfamiliar with the cautionary tale "The Sorcerer's Apprentice," find it and read it, or watch the Disney cartoon which is a segment of the Oscar winning animated feature, Fantasia. This should demonstrate why you need to be a master and not merely raise someone else's wand and mutter incantations.

Storytelling is neither for sissies nor for dummies. Do not go into the trade because you were not good at math or science in school. The differences between art and science tend to be exaggerated and wishful thinking anyway. Making good art is not any easier than making good science.

Storytellers need to be clear-thinkers in pursuit of fuzzy truths, since no matter who or where the characters in a story are, at bottom, we are addressing real people leading real lives, and life is rarely simple or straightforward. A story is, in a sense, attempting to resolve life's little unresolvable paradoxes such as death. But perhaps that is for a more sophisticated book. Here we will try to be practical.

As a way of demonstrating how the internal logic of a story guides writers toward making storytelling decisions that work, we return to our example protagonist, who we last left in an alley to fall, or not to fall, for the honeyed lips of a succubus. So, let us change that – abracadabra! Let us shoot the protagonist instead, but maybe not in an alley. No, he is shot and left to die on the glorious blood-soaked field of battle but, what do you know, he is nursed back to health by, who else but a beautiful woman. (She is back again.)

Being shot in a battle and left to bleed to death is now the game changer. This is the incident that gets us into Act II, where everything that happens, happens – meaning where the plot happens. The shooter has stepped into the role of an antagonist. It is he who shunts the train on to a different track, but we will never know anything else about the patriotic fellow. We do not have to even see him. That is the way it is with some antagonists. Poor guys.

The woman, however, now becomes the female lead cast as, what was referred to during the golden era of Hollywood, "the other woman." But she is no longer a brazen hussy. She is now the co-protagonist and the "love-interest." No longer in a supporting role, she has been promoted.

We will now remake the first protagonist into a wounded Union Captain near death after, forget a battle, a dastardly ambush during the Civil War. We will make the co-protagonist the recently married wife of a Confederate Colonel. We want to remain practical, and for entirely practical reasons, we will make her more attractive and alluring than the perfectly good wife the noble/dashing Union Captain has left at home with his two children. We throw in his children to up the ante, which, in the golden era was sometimes called "spicing it up." Now we have a man with normal responsibilities in an abnormal situation, the Civil War.

This new spiced-up situation transitions us into Act II. Of course, all the situations in Act II are subject to change, but they must change in a manner that takes us to where light can be cast on the meaning of life.

Sorry, I can think of no way of saying it that is less grandiose: **Storytelling is either about the meaning of life or it is poor storytelling.**

The situations that antagonists create to challenge the protagonists in Act II should not change only to maintain audience interest, although they must accomplish that as well. If interest is all that is accomplished scene after scene, eventually that will lead

to audience let-down. (Which is bad.) The audience needs to be transported to at least a plausible meaning of some aspect of their own life journey. We could simply remove the love interest's clothes if all we wanted was to keep the audience engaged with what is on the screen. We very well might do that at some future point. But we will not do it now, and we will not do that gratuitously, just to engage audience prurience. For one thing, that is too cheap and easy, and so beneath us. Much more importantly, we will ask ourselves first, **to what ends any given "bit of business" leads.**

As an aside, sex in a story, by itself, is just another "bit of business," the same as a robbery or a little murder. A sex scene also has to be on the story spine. **Every situation or scene in every Act II must function as a means to an end, and so must force the protagonist to make moral choices, and act on them. Or not.** (Unfortunately, more than a few writers and filmmakers do not seem to get this message.) Bearing that in mind, we will skip the sex, for now.

Moral choices, however, we cannot leave for later. And it would be poor storytelling to make those moral choices easy for our handsome Captain. That would be boring for the storyteller, and for the audience. Thus, our new starting situation for Act II has a noble/dashing male lead, with the dutiful, doting (if not quite as pretty) wife back home. Then, to spice up the pot even more, we will make it that the gorgeous nurse is under the impression that her husband, the Confederate Colonel, is dead. Thus, the co-protagonists are both traumatized by the war. They are both lonely, and both desperate for some light in all this darkness. In other words, they are vulnerable to love.

The above situation now roughed out, we have left ourselves many options for what can happen in Act II. We can choose from a huge variety of plot points, but thankfully, the selection is limited by the internal-logic of the story. We get to choose plot points from what best serves our two masters, the external one being audience interest, the internal one being the story theme. The internal logic is driven by the story theme. Our theme concerns doing what feels right and even "good" versus doing what our sense of social duty and morality tells us is right. This is dicey and messy, as it should be. Do we sacrifice what feels good for what is right? Do we sacrifice an in-the-face now for a possible later? When is that appropriate, if it is ever appropriate? Always? Sometimes? Here? Now? What governs such choices? What should govern these moral choices? What you have been taught? What is instinctual? We need to spend time pondering these weighty matters. This will save us time, in the medium run.

All situations in Act II need to present moral quandaries. This particular quandary, however, is as common as dirt. The audience faces it often in their own lives, even if rarely on such a grand scale. The scale, however, serves the story by bringing everything into vivid, high resolution. Immediate gratification versus long-term happiness, or at least wellbeing, is a nattering dog constantly nipping at our heels. But we cannot simply pit short term pleasure against long term happiness and say morality wins. We also cannot do the opposite. Morality is one of the things at core in all tales; but this will not be a melodrama, or a tale designed to elevate the moral fiber of our audience, just as it equally will not be an invitation to what is bawdy and licentious.

What happens in our Act II cannot come down to a momentary lapse of judgment in the fog of war or an all too human bump on the road of an otherwise moral life. The audience will be bored if this is all that is depicted. No, we are crafting a romance. We need more. They have to fall for each other, and fall hard. It must be true love, not just pleasure. It must seem to be that at least. Otherwise, the story would have no lasting traction with the audience. This is about a Big Issue, about sacrifice, honor, fidelity, and people rubbed raw and tender by extraordinarily brutal circumstances. That allows us to examine what is really important and do some sorting from what we are taught is really important, such as patriotism, or keeping your marriage vows. It is not that we, as storytellers, will make that kind of judgment for the audience. We are no preachers. But we will put conventional thinking under the microscope and poke it. One element that gives us license to do that is that war, hideous as it is, is also a convention, and look at what that has led to. Perhaps other things we have been told about right and wrong are also, shall we say, a little dodgy? What is it that we really owe others and what is it that we really owe ourselves, and can they ever be reconciled? A Big Issue indeed.

It is best that before we proceed into the deep woods of Act II, we do our best to wrestle it to the ground. (Of course, we will never win that wrestling match, not entirely; but as storytellers, we are bound to try.)

Questions to consider for our Civil War lovers' story include, how much sacrifice is required of a person? Surely, these two fundamentally decent human beings have sacrificed enough. What do our co-protagonists owe themselves? Everything? Nothing? Why?

One thing is clear: To get at a Big Issue, the personal stakes for the protagonists, who, like all protagonists, are surrogates for our audience, need to be very high.

It is always about doing the right thing in the deep woods of Act II. But frequently it is not easy to know what that is –not in life or for our protagonists. We want to make the going very hard for them. We do not want clarity in a story until the climax, but we do want an overall sense of escalating risk until then. So what is being risked here? This is a Big Question that we, as storytellers, need to address early on. Why? **Because the audience needs a sense of what is being risked from the beginning of Act II.**

It is for this reason that we might have an early scene in Act II in which the Union Captain flashes back to his wife and children as he is lying in his own blood, just before he blacks out. In this way, the audience will learn that he still loves the woman back home but, alas, he is no longer in love with her. On the other hand, he is certainly loves his children. Bam! Hits the audience right in the heart.

When he wakes, he finds himself gazing into the crystal-line eyes of the woman/angel who has nursed him back to life.

I have to admit that there is nothing astonishingly new here. There does not need to be for a story to be successful. A canny storyteller can squeeze juice from the old bugaboo delineated above forever.

Now, to up the ante even more, this man and this woman, for whom the circumstances of war (and the craft of the storyteller) have contrived to put together, let them be loyal to opposite sides in the war and passionately so. He is a dyed-in-the-wool Yankee and she is a fervent "Johnny Reb." This serves as shorthand for our audience, demonstrating that these two are not radical outsiders and are conventional in their loyalties –as is, no doubt, the target audience.

It might be a little over the top for storytellers to thank the Good Lord for war, but it is the war in this instance that shakes things up for our little tale, and that is a good thing. Our war is, in fact, a pig-headed, fratricidal civil war, and that, for our storytelling purposes, is extremely convenient. There had been one country that you were loyal to, but now you might find yourself fighting that same country. You were brothers and now you might find yourself on opposite sides. You might find yourself killing a friend. A civil war is a war on steroids.

Conventional loyalties often fall apart in any war, or they are redefined as in the Civil War romance being toyed with here. How fortunate then that challenging conventions is something storytellers can employ to shed light on what really matters in life and what might not.

Then there are conventional truths. We all know that conventional truths are not necessarily true, but in normal times this is often papered over. In our case, fashioning our co-protagonists as normal, conventional people, albeit abnormally good looking, and then placing them into an existential crisis serves to make them question their handed-down values and loyalties. Their straying from convention also helps to make them more sympathetic to the target audience. What we are really doing is challenging norms in the interest of truths.

Heroes need to be sympathetic. Heroes can be aliens, but they need to be appealing aliens, such as an alien called ET in the movie of the same name. Aliens cannot be alien to who we are or who the audience is.

But who are we really? This too is at the heart of storytelling. This is why setting the story during the Civil War creates a convenient situation for the characters to be tested on their conventional values. Pretenses will no longer suffice here. For this reason, we have added into the mix an unfulfilling marriage –in fact, as soon we will learn, two unfulfilling marriages. These co-protagonists are both conventionally loyal to their marriages just as they are conventionally patriotic. Neither of them is a maverick. That might be for a different tale. It is important for the audience to appreciate in this story, however, that these are not people who lightly shirk their responsibilities. After all, they are heroes, but they are also human heroes in love, who have fallen into a temporary Eden. It has to be temporary because if they fell into a lasting Eden, we would already be in Act III. Still, we now know that the setting where this love affair takes place probably should be idyllic, like a garden. This is not, of course, the only possible setting, but our choices have been greatly narrowed, because we are confined to the demands of our story theme. A garden evokes renewal, new life, and hope –the opposite of the war. It makes sense to drop our lovers into Eden 2.0. No?

Since we are in the middle of Act II wherein we have contrived that the war still wages in the wings, this would be a garden under threat. The war will, in fact, creep ever closer, serving to make the audience suitably nervous – which is exactly what we want. Again, we do not need to wrack our brains. Knowing your theme makes the entire story writing process enormously easier.

107

The theme (what your story is about) functions as a compass, pointing the direction toward what all the major elements of a story must be like –including what settings, events, and order of events leading to the climax are more likely to maximize the effectiveness of Act II.

The effect we are after, mind you, is on the audience. After the curtain falls, we want to leave them with more clarity about some Big Issue in their lives. It does not matter if they are aware of our little contrivances or not. It matters that we are.

When Mozart was asked how he could write his music so effortlessly, his reply was that he had a pipeline to a divine source. I do not feel he was being arrogant, or even fanciful. This described his subjective experience as a composer. Similarly, the storytelling process can feel to the master storyteller as if he or she were taking dictation.

Supposedly, Mozart was able to tell a joke and write the counter-bassoon part to what will become a great symphony simultaneously. If so, few other human beings can equal such a boast. But even Mozart had to occasionally struggle. (I mean, one would hope!) There will still be obstacles that interrupt the flow of writing fiction, but now there emerges a methodology for how to surmount those obstacles. **What is called "writer's block" will be a rare event for those who write with a story theme guiding them.**

The theme(s) is only laid down in Act I. It needs to be explored and "proved" in Act II. We are on the hunt for nothing less than truth, and both love and war can serve as catalysts to help separate "signal" from "noise." But in this particular tale, the war will remain secondary. This will be primarily a romance set against destruction, cruelty, desperation, and topsy-turvy turmoil, and set on a tranquil island.

There is no reason to worry that choosing the love aspect over the war aspect will be detrimental. The Civil War was only the backdrop for one of the greatest Hollywood romances –and box-office hits– of all time, Gone with the Wind.

Picasso said, "Good artists copy, great artists steal." I would add, "If you gotta steal –and you gotta– steal from the greats." Steal shamelessly, but do not be a mimic. Make what you steal yours, just as those you stole from had to do.

All themes have been exploited before, and so has ours. Questions remain, however, even if you are writing Romeo and Juliet and your name is Will. Here is one for our story theme: does "love conquer all," or does "the world" (the war) compromise all? Under that age-old dialectic, we are having two lonely, exhausted, discouraged people fall hard for each other. Anyone in such a situation would be looking for safe harbor from the storm, but these two have stumbled into Eden. The audience knows that this cannot last, but they still need to be reminded. Reminding them functions as a poke with a sharp stick and keeps them on edge –which, again, is desirable.

Keeping in mind that what happens in Act II –not some of it but all of it– is informed by the story theme, we would like to believe in that theme; except here, we have our two Big Ideas facing off against each other. That is messy, but so is a human life. Most of us would probably like to believe that "Love conquers all" but we also all know that this is not always true; sometimes, other maxims prevail instead, like, for example: "To the victor go the spoils." In the competition that is also a life, a millionaire can serve as a stand-in for a "victor" and the person he or she is slated to marry could conceivably constitute "the spoils." Knowing that the theme in a story needs to be wrapped in human skin, and the humans then set on a journey, we now have major hints about the development of the back-story for the female lead.

There can be little doubt that "true love" often seems shaky in the light of practical experience. Someone in real life might choose, or maybe his or her parents might choose for them, a millionaire for a spouse. Circumstance may make the pragmatic choice the only reasonable choice. You might marry someone who is not your "true love," and yet, arguably, choosing practicality over "true love" could be the smart choice. The classic 1950s Hollywood movie, How To Marry A Millionaire, explores this idea with co-protagonist femme fatales, Betty Grable, Marilyn Monroe, and Lauren Bacall as the "gold diggers."

But does love trump money? After all, marriages of convenience have worked out serviceably in real life for centuries, and in many cultures arranged marriages remain the custom. You might argue, something is lost, but something is also often gained. Many people seem to nod their acquiescence for the practical approach, and yet, whatever the case for or against pragmatic marriages, "Love conquers all" seems to be what almost all audiences want to believe. Few of us are entirely practical when it comes to love. Thousands of hugely popular Hollywood movies have been constructed upon this quandary –and maybe even dozens of good ones. Audiences everywhere cheerlead for the "Love conquers all" ideal. This sentiment appears to be truly universal, and so too its opposite, "True love may not be enough." (Romeo and Juliet)

This is why we will encumber our leading lady, whom we have decided is a young woman in glorious full blossom, in a marriage of convenience to a much older man. (More details to come. We are still crafting our tale, allowing our themes to guide us.)

Usually, all you need is an antagonistic force to switch the train on to the desirable track, via storytelling. Any old feud or war will do, but there are countless other situations to bring this Big Issue into sharp focus. That said, we also need something to challenge conventional thinking and reveal a little about what the Irish poet William Butler Yeats referred to as "the time before the world began." Our temporary Eden can serve that function quite well.

The situation where two people fall deeply in love but social rules seem to force them apart, powers hundreds of movies and novels world-wide every year. We too can harness the tension inherent in this situation to power our second act. That is why we will give this man and this woman a walloping dose of pure animal chemistry. We will use animal passions to break the chains of conventionality. Conveniently, the sexy bits of Act II cater to the audience's innate prurient curiosity. At least in a tale, there is nothing intrinsically wrong with a little lustful animalism, but you cannot throw just anything into a stew and expect it to be a success. This particular ingredient –the sexy bits– has to also pass the internal logic muster.

Remember, we want to get at what makes life worth living; what has lasting and not just ephemeral value. There needs to be something linking to what is, or what can be, transcendent in "the little animal act." It is transcendence that a proper romance alludes to. Properly speaking, a sex scene, like all scenes, is just an event. Good stories do not merely describe or portray events; they have to get at what is important. Events in Act II need to add up. We will not break this rule.

A storyteller throws into the stew whatever makes a better tasting stew. Too many ingredients spoil any stew, as do the wrong ingredients. There should be no gratuitous ingredients in a story stew. None. Gratuitous sex, gratuitous violence, gratuitous anything, is symptomatic of weak storytelling. But for our tale, this ingredient is not gratuitous. We will utilize it to evoke "the time before the world was made." For our purposes, despite the political differences of our protagonists, despite different loyalties and backgrounds, despite their mutual and often conventional sense of honor, nature must win out for love to win out –at least for a plot point or two. A romance does not have to have a "Hollywood ending." Stay tuned...

Simply put, once our man is shot and left to die, it is enough violence to get us into Act II. Any more would be gratuitous. This Act II does not need heads being smashed like pumpkins or limbs being severed from healthy young bodies. This is not Saving Private Ryan. We will nevertheless reserve the possibility of violence for later.

Meanwhile, most of us over the age of puberty know what raging hormones are about. Hormones threaten to "conquer all." Quite often we are fighting our "natures" because we are convinced that succumbing to our urges is not conducive to human happiness. But it requires considerable effort to override our natural urges. That is a large part of conventional child rearing. Our audience will expect nothing less of our co-protagonists, which is why the sex in our plot will occur only after they both try to resist. That will go a good distance to credit the protagonists as honorable, and when they finally do what comes naturally, we see them as subject to the usual human foibles –just like our target audience. So, again, **the sexy stuff is not gratuitous, not here. We toss it into the stew with aplomb, because we now understand what this particular plot device does on our story spine.**

Nevertheless, we cannot end our story with, "Wham, bam, thank you, ma'am." For one thing, it would be tawdry, meaning empty of meaning. It would put us off the story spine and off theme. A scene where they finally fall into each other's arms, with or without graphic sex, earns its right to exist only if it serves the needs of the next scene. We are still building our Act II. Perhaps we also need to throw in a sage –say a quirky midwife or greying country doctor (someone to be the adult)–to help us along by evoking the theme, clothed in kindly advice. (That was the main purpose of the character, Mammy, in Gone With The Wind.)

So far, however, not enough light has been generated by our plot to illuminate our theme. As storytellers, we do not need to shine a light so strong that it vanquishes all darkness. We do not want to blind with our light. We need shadow to recognize the light. We love shadow, but we do need light. So ... "Let there be light." Maybe just a flickering match in all that darkness. The audience deserves that moment of meaning –and maybe a hint of the possibility of fulfillment. Just a general direction. Just the possibility more than suffices, for any tale. The audience needs hope flashed in front of their hungry eyes. Then we, as storytellers, can take it away.

Or not. That will be for Act III. Meanwhile, our co-protagonists also need some hope in the dire situation we have put them into just as our audience needs hope in the situations they are dealing with in their daily lives.

We want our audience to think, "Ah, so that's how it could be!" Then most of our job will be done. We need to show them light, even if we intend to extinguish it, as Shakespeare does time and time again in many of his better plays –but never more so than in *Romeo and Juliet*.

Therefore, the physical situation our main characters face will have to become more dire –that is, if the physical is to serve as the glue for something more important and meaningful. We want our tale to transcend the physical, which, in itself, is without meaning in the same way that a rock is without meaning. Not that there is anything wrong with a rock, or nature generally, but the job of the storyteller is to invest the rock with meaning, such as through metaphor: "A relationship built upon granite."

Of course, this one probably cannot be built upon granite. It would be unwise. Better that it is built in quicksand, or at least it seems to be. It can last, but for our theme, we do not need it to last. It better serves our purposes if it is doomed like Romeo and Juliet are doomed by "the world." We do need the relationship, such that it is, to evoke that "world before the earth was made." We need that to be earned by this man and this woman as a meaningful reminder to the audience who knows damn well that any good relationship does not come easily. This is not The Simpsons, with its adorably comically flawed family built upon middle class granite. That suits their storytelling; meaning, it serves their themes. But our story needs a sense of fragility and the specter of doom, or rather "boom," as the war approaches our protagonists' little Eden.

Why can't we depict their relationship as solid? Because the essence of a good romance story is that the relationship remains in peril, at least until Act III. Even with bawdy bits thrown in, the relationship needs to infer something transcendent. Can just having a strong boy-girl relationship substitute for meaning in our lives, really? Not in real life and not in good storytelling. We cannot just slot in a solid emotional relationship and intimacy that functions as a fortress against everything that is bad, add a little hot sex so that everyone knows they also have chemistry, and leave them to their happi-ly-ever-after. Where would that get us?

No. In real life, adults earn their happiness. Happiness is serious business. In a romantic story, if we are depicting what seems to be a good relationship, we need to demonstrate how that is earned. The Simpsons manages to do that, in one way or another, in every episode. For the purposes of our romance, as fleshed out so far, we need to imply that in a better world, these two wounded humans could be good for each other. Maybe they would walk arm in arm into the golden sunset many years later in that better world.

But they have been cast in the world that we have made for them. We have made for them a little war. In our Act II, their relationship will have its ups and downs. We want the audience to think that just maybe these two have stumbled into the Garden Of Eden. And we should bring up the violins because that sense of hope and hap-piness needs to build until harsh reality breaks into their garden to kick their pretty behinds and test the fabric of both of their characters as well as the relationship.

The tests in Act Two will need to strip everything away that obscures the truth about the protagonists and their situation. What is left only should be what is important. It is what is important that needs to be at risk. When we test their romantic relationship, what we are really testing is the serious business of happiness. We need to contrive our situation, our plot, our Act II, so that it does precisely that. And the audience needs to be right there with us.

Can you see that we are building a map? Can you see how having the map makes depicting "the hero's journey" much easier? Do you appreciate that we are not just outlining plot points on four-by-six cards here? No, a map is different. It is more than that and less than that, but it will inform you about the core of your tale, and then plot points probably will occur to you, seemingly out of the ether. Stick them on the wall, shuffle them, replace some, take some away, add some more ... if it is helpful. There is nothing wrong with this methodology, commonly taught around the world. If that is your methodology, get to it. But allow the map to coalesce out of the ether first.

Are you getting a sense of the mechanics behind the miracle of storytelling? Good. But first, you need to wrestle your theme to the ground. After that, the mechanics will emerge organically.

The game changer is understanding what your story is really about. What it is really about is your story theme or themes. In the end, all stories are "representative or symbolic of something else, especially something abstract." That is the dictionary definition

of a metaphor. Every tale is a metaphor. So what is your story about?

It tends to be more efficient to do the wrestling with the theme before you start writing, but it is not necessary. Some of us muddle around, sniffing the ground like truffle pigs, attempting to identify our meaning. We all have our personal ways to get at our themes. Whatever works. As long as it gets the job done.

Learn to write "from theme" and you will find that making fiction will happen as if it was magic. This is because it is magic, but the magic happens after you learn the trick. You gotta learn it to earn it.

So, getting back to our example: true love. Really? Will it prevail? Can it prevail in these circumstances? Question that idea throughout the entirety of your machinations in Act II. If the holy grail is true love, how does that make the hero's journey worth the undertaking? Identify the "why" of it. Or is this to be just another one of those comforting stories we tell ourselves, and then tell our children to create the illusion of meaning in our lives? The audience demands answers to big questions even though they might not be aware that they are asking.

Luckily, storytellers need not supply definitive answers; only illumination.

In this imaginary Act II, we are pitting the maxim "Love Conquers All" against the maxim, "War Destroys All." More prosaically, this boils down to the proposition that "real life" intrudes to decimate our precious ideals and values. We are probing that premise. We inflate "real life" in the story: We simplify it, exaggerate it, and amplify it through war. The war, then, is also a metaphor. But we know the identity of the dragon we are after. Powerful universal themes are being exploited as harsh reality is set against the translucent gossamer of romance.

This is fertile soil, but, for something to grow in it, there needs to be evolution. Nothing in nature evolves without an existential threat. So, our lovers, having taken the plunge; having taken on emotional risk; having coalesced true love out of the ether; and having taken on a risk made even riskier because of the perilous uncertainty of war; now must face an existential threat of our choosing. We can add this via the agency of an antagonist. If we come up with one, the audience will be compelled to see how it works out for the two romantic heroes.

The audience already understands that, sometimes, bad things happen to good people, such as when a person is shot. They understand that, sometimes, good things happen to good people, such as when the good person is nursed back to health by someone with whom he proceeds to fall head-over-heels in love with. In fact, here, the feeling turns out to be mutual. How good is that?

The audience knows that stuff happens. So what? That these two live happily ever after would be just a summation in Act III. Or not. The existential question for storytellers is, would it matter to the audience? Where is the meat between the buns of Act I and Act III? In Act II, in any and all stories, theory needs to be tested in practice. Once we, as storytellers, have put flesh on those bones – once we have credibly brought these Big Ideas to life and properly tested them through the agency of our antagonist– it can end either way for our lovers. As storytellers, either way can be effective for us.

It is not enough for a good chef to simply cook a goose. How did the goose taste? Did the customers enjoy the meal? As a good storyteller, you will be asking similar questions. How did the story go down? Did they feel they wasted their money and time? The audience might, for example, witness once and again a nominal Adam and a nominal Eve getting hoofed out of Eden. They may be sad for our lovers. In fact, they should be. We need our audience to be rooting for our protagonists. That is part of our job. We can disappoint our audience, but they should never be disappointed with our story.

This-happens-and-then-that-happens is not a story. A series of events does not satisfy the definition of a story, even if it might constitute a plot. Insight into those events does. The audience would feel cheated otherwise. They are there for insight. So far, the above can only serve as the beginning of our story. We are not even halfway through Act II.

True, a lot has already happened in our plot, but that would not keep a crafty storyteller from teasing the audience further by dangling the foolish notion that it is likely to end well for the co-protagonists. This we might do, but only if we've done the other job –infusing our tale with meaning– which results in the audience waiting in uneasy and pregnant anticipation for the other shoe to drop. You want to do both. This is how you glue an audience to the screen or a reader to page after page after page.

The audience should feel unease in the pits of their stomachs throughout most of Act II. A master storyteller will do what is needed to preserve that feeling. For how long? For just the right number of notes. (Thanks again, Mozart!)

The effective storyteller knows when there is no meaning to the tale, even if what happened so far is thrilling

119

enough to have captivated the audience. The effective storyteller will be working throughout Act II to provide illumination. **The meaning, however, should not be apparent until near the end of Act II. Effectively, once the meaning gets through, your tale is through.** For the term "meaning," we can substitute the phrase, "What it's about."

The storyteller for this Act II, therefore, might want to reconstrue the situation this way: The co-protagonists really do find true love. Lucky them. They have just stumbled upon it, like the blind hog that occasionally finds an acorn. It nevertheless strikes them as a miraculous stroke of good fortune. It actually turns out to be fortunate, therefore, that the dashing, young Union Captain has been shot and left for dead. It is a blessing in disguise as it leads directly to him being gifted with new life by the beautiful co-protagonist. For a while that is – for so many notes and beats in Act II that all seems right in the world– until it is not. Why? Because that is how life tends to be. Also, all being right in the world is not a story. The supposition goes against our experience in the world. Ours is a tale aimed at adults, not children. We have identified our target demographic and will not insult them by treating them like children. We must find a monkey wrench to toss into the machinery.

When any audience is left muttering, "So what?" at the end of a tale, the storyteller has failed to deliver the goods. A twist on the situation is needed to get at that what. The internal logic of storytelling demands it. A good moment for the twist, in our particular storytelling exercise, might be just after the lovers have satiated their passions for the first time and are lying heart-to-heart, limbs intertwined. Alternatively, we might linger just a little longer, feeding the audience a scene or two, allowing them to savor the hope that this relationship might really have legs –that there is hope for them within the sanctuary of romantic love– until the blessed moment when the storyteller kicks the legs out from under the audience.

No good Act II leaves anyone satisfied for long. Save the satisfaction for Act III. So let's make changes. Abracadabra! The beautiful young widow turns out to not be a widow. This little twist is meant to propel the audience toward the moment of insight, revelation, transcendence, and payoff. Thus, her husband, battle scarred, not so handsome, grayer, and decidedly older than our dashing Union Captain, rides up.

Et voila ... our main characters and, in tandem, the audience, are reminded that they are all still in the pickle jar, and are, in fact, about to have the lid twisted on even tighter. Their private little Eden has just popped like an iridescent soap bubble. Bam! Right out of Eden they go!

If we are really clever devils, however, we might choose not to make the Confederate Colonel the standard, snarling, black-hearted villain. Instead, working again within the internal logic of this tale, we will render him a gray-haired aristocrat chappie –more honorable, more polite, more experienced, more self-assured, more refined, and perhaps even kinder, than both the Union Captain and his cuckolding wife. Yes, the edges have been burnished off the dear old man. There is much to be admired in him, and there is still fire within the hearth, even if there is snow on the roof. Frightening, isn't it? Life pitting good people against good people?

We will need to make it clear that his young wife really does admire and love her husband –but alas, more as a father figure than a lover. Bearing in mind the storytelling purpose of what we have now concocted, the woman, recently a bride, needs to feel more than a dollop of shame to remain likable. She must now muster the strength to distance herself emotionally –or try to– from the handsome, virile young man with whom she had so recently, passionately lain.

This is now a situation in which our Southern gentleman has every right to demand satisfaction. In fact, conventional honor of the era would demand nothing less. Also, if the kindly, wise, and war-weary husband will not function as a catalyst, what damn use is he? This well-meaning antagonist must defend his honor. This would be the conventional sentiment of the era. People are honor bound by their conventions, are they not?

Meanwhile, there is room for a little back-story here about the young lady, or maybe that could have been slotted in earlier: Perhaps the young lady's mother died in child-birth, and her father started drinking. That, and bad luck, led to bankruptcy and her father's suicide. Alas, having become a destitute orphan, things were looking bad for this former child of privilege –until that bittersweet moment when a silver-haired Colonel proposed to her. The two were married, let us say, a year before the war, when she was, let us say, seventeen years old.

We could dream up other back-stories, but all of them would have to function as a discourse on the subject of how the "ideal" confronts the "real." So let's keep this one. It is the kind of nasty business that gets to the heart of our "what's-it-about." If this (or any) story point did not accomplish that goal, it would not just be a waste of time; it would have a fair chance of knocking the story completely off the tracks. It would weaken our tale.

The audience would be muttering their dissatisfaction as they trailed out of the theater.

Practically speaking, as you write, you may not have figured out every angle. You might come to realize that you missed an opportunity to make the story a little better. **But if you understand the internal logic of your story, you can easily go back, add something, remove something, change something, re-jigger a situation, and it should slot right back in, requiring few additional adjustments before or after the change. If, on the other hand, you failed to understand your story theme, or you did not really have one, there would be no internal logic to guide you.** It would be unlikely that you could improve matters much, whatever fiddling you did.

If every change you make seems to mean you need major changes in other places, you are probably on the wrong track. A major re-think of what your story is really about would be in order.

Back to the story, and the fresh surprise of sympathy for this antagonist ... Damn it, she is still his wife, and he had cherished her, provided for her abundantly, and loved her. Her new lover, to make it more insulting to him, is on the opposite side in that great miserable reality, the American Civil War. The rift is deep, and it stands as a gulf between them just as much as she does. But she makes it personal. We are chugging up the hill in our Civil War train towards the climax. This turn of events augurs that now it is just about the time for lovely violence. The internal logic of our tale seems to guide us this way. The audience has been basking in the pleasant little romantic bubble just about long enough. They need a jolt of harsh reality. In fact, they would appreciate it. Lightning flashes are, after all, a means of illumination, and so can be the muzzle flash of a cannon.

But remember, we are clever foxes, we storytellers. This is also a good place in the plot to put a twist on the twist.

First, we will remind the audience just how miserable this period in U.S. history was and how difficult it would be for this Colonel to gracefully accept this situation in which a Yankee has become his wife's lover. Perhaps we will go back a few pages in the script or novel, and insert a detail to drive the point home: let's say the Colonel is missing an arm. Or the arm can just dangle uselessly and indignantly. And, what do you know? It is his shooting arm.

Perhaps we will insert a new scene that graphically depicts how the Colonel lost the arm, preferably in some valiant way – he cannot just be drunk and fall off his horse. Of course, he loses the arm to a Union cannon or a cavalry saber. In this scene, the Confederate side is vastly outnumbered (as they really were towards the late stages of the conflict). Rebel-grey clad bodies are strewn all around. Mud, straw, blood, smoke and flame, hideous twisted corpses of men and horses. Rigor mortis and all of that. Then, one desperate last charge into the flaming maw of black powder hell, led by the valiant grey-haired warrior ... Yes, now we are splitting the audience's loyalties.

Here the old guy almost dies just as the young Captain almost died. (That is called "parallel construction.") Maybe he should have died. Maybe that would have been kinder considering that now his side is just about vanquished, and he has made it back home with General Sherman nipping at his heels only to find that his gorgeous young wife has fallen for a young, handsome Yankee.

So here he is. Clearly, he had not perished in battle as the young woman had believed. Secretly hoped perhaps? Had she always been secretly pining for true romance? Had there been, deep within her, a feeling of relief, now that the old man she had married was supposedly dead? Apparently, there was. But, apparently, he is not dead. Bam! Life sometimes takes this kind of startling turn.

Please note: The true romance in the story can also be viewed as life released to finally take its natural course in a very unnatural setting, which is war. Wars tend to do that. That is one reason they are as fun to write about as sex. And here we have both: sex and violence! Will not the crowd be pleased?

But maybe this new turn of events should not be so cut and dried. Let us make it that she had more wanted to believe that he was dead, than she had real reason to believe. Maybe there always had been a decent chance that he was alive, but she had seized on the possibility that he was not. She is young, after all. Fate had foisted the old goat on her. She wants her own Act II.

So, if that is what we feel is needed, we now go back in the tale and ensure that she had no definitive proof that he had died. Arguably, as his wife, she should have waited until she knew her husband really was dead, especially since he was good, kindly, wise, and generous. And boy, do we want to make sure that the audience views him this way. She, however, is a young, impetuous, passionate woman in full flower with a husband twice her age, in a war, with her romantic ideals of happiness quashed. We want the audience to be rooting for her too. This is the type of quandary that keeps the audience on the edge of their seats.

Again it is the war. And war is hell, but as fiction writers, we should be thankful for a little murder and a nice war. Murder, war, and a dash of sex allowed Shakesphere to shed light on universal themes. Who are we mere mortals to argue with genius?

All this new detail and back-story adds peril and predicament. It complicates the situation, muddies the moral waters, and serves the rather good function of leaving our young wife with conflicting loyalties. Now that the good Colonel is back, the young woman is torn between two lovers, and two different kinds of love: what the classical Greeks named Eros –romantic, passionate love– and Philia –affectionate, deep, and abiding, friendly love.

Both of these men are decent enough people. It is just this damn war!

Why are they all decent, you ask? Because if these people were not so darn decent, it would weaken our story. So we make them decent. See?

The time is ripe for the older man to demand "the satisfaction of a duel, sir!" No one, including the young wife, including the audience, doubts how this would likely end. That missing or dead arm we inserted into the tale serves to underscore the reality. We have now arrived at a critical point in the plot when the young man, who has fallen utterly in love with the Colonel's beautiful wife, will almost certainly have to kill him. The Colonel, in fact, demands it. First he loses the war, and then her? Intolerable!

The duel is to be at sunrise. The night before is cordial. At some point, perhaps when the wife leaves to put on the kettle, it might be a good idea that our Colonel reveals to the younger man that Sherman's Army is marching in their direction and burning everything before it. It is only a matter of time until they will arrive at this plantation. This is new information. It comes as good news to the Union Captain, and he cannot conceal his elation.

The conversation shifts to the key of tense when the honorable Colonel accuses the Union Army of having no honor. He warns the Union Captain that they will certainly pillage and destroy the plantation. The conquering soldiers will also do what conquering armies always do to the beautiful wives of opposing officers. He has already lost everything. His wife will once again be left destitute, and probably worse than that is about to befall her. He seeks a pledge from the Captain that he will restore his wife's honor in the conventional sense, by marrying her. He reasons that as the wife of a Yankee officer, she will be safe. Probably it is best to mention the deal over whiskey and cheroots.

Now comes an opportunity to put a twist on the twist. Our Captain would have gladly agreed to what the Colonel asked of him. But lest we forget –he already has his own wife and children. So he too is torn between loyalties. That was no accident. We planted the rat in the lover's Eden for this version of our imaginary scene, and it's been scratching around in the background all along.

One thing, though: The young man certainly is not about to spill the beans to the Colonel, is he? Murdering him might well be more merciful.

If we are doing our job right, this monkey wrench thrown into the machinery should keep the audience properly conflicted and on the edge of their seats, desperate to know how our protagonists get out of this pickle jar.

It is a quandary that might be exaggerated for storytelling reasons, but it is not substantively different from situations most people find themselves in. How much does a decent, responsible person need to sacrifice to lead an honorable life? How many of our dreams must we compromise in the name of conventional honor? Should we shed the manacles of convention given the opportunity? What would be the value in doing that? Not all conventions are "mere conventions." Some conventions arise from virtue. Maybe it sounds like an adventure, but maybe we should not go on it. Maybe we must maintain honor, conventional or not, or it all quickly goes to hell in a handbasket. Civilization, stability, the social bonds that hold us all together, etc. all of that.

Thick soup, this, but soup that you cannot necessarily purchase around the corner. That is the point. That is why it might be interesting. That is why we, the storytellers, muddy the moral waters: to make our protagonists as fully human as we can manage, warts and all, so the audience can relate.

Meanwhile, that young woman, having been cast out of heaven and into the very pit of hell, weeps in the kitchen beside a boiling tea kettle. ...

What to do? What to do? The terrible lovely quandary sends us hurtling headlong into the climax of our imaginary Act II.

4. Setting The Stakes, Raising The Peril

Our Two Heroes in the Pickle Jar. How War Can Be a Good Thing?

Most storytelling dilemmas can be described generally as choosing between opposing maxims: "He who hesitates is lost" versus "Look before you leap." As for our instructive exercise, we have arrived at yet another for our critical plot point: "Damned if you do, damned if you don't." We have stuffed our protagonists into the pickle jar and sealed it tight. This is as it must be.

Remember, in the latest interaction, they both have taken marriage vows. Marriage is a central principle of their society. So is sacrificing your own happiness, or perhaps even your own life, at times, for the "greater good." Remember, they are both honorable, or at least, they both try to remain honorable in a very challenging situation. If the dashing Yankee Captain and the vibrant young wife of an aging Confederate colonel are portrayed as fairly decent people, they might "hesitate" before they "leap." They might look at what is before them, consider what the conventional wisdom views as fundamental to moral and social wellbeing, and follow the social convention for "the greater good."

Lofty words. If they did that, they would have to part ways and return to their respective spouses; and, in the Captain's case as well, to his children. The young woman would still be facing what she is facing. But in so doing, they would lose their chance at "true love," and the audience is denied the satisfying, "They lived happily ever after" ending. What to do?

It might be that the only resolution for how we have crafted this tale is that the young woman has to die. Sorry.

The protagonists could preserve their honor and take what is widely regarded as the high road, but the story would still need to shed light on whether any of that has real value. Are these merely social conventions, which often are ephemeral? (Consider the demise of the institution of marriage in our times before you answer that question.) **If our tale ended here without resolution, the audience would be left unsatisfied. Act III would fail. Therefore, the tale cannot finish here. Our honor as story-smiths is at stake.**

So, how to wrap it up? The answer always lies in returning to our story theme. War is a social convention just as much as marriage is it not. We have imagined a tale that dares take on the idea that true morality –precepts that really do promote human happiness and well-being– can sometimes conflict with conventional morality, which includes both marriage and war. We are taking advantage of the tendency war has to expose hypocrisy. War can let the light in, which is possibly why many people are at least unconsciously drawn to it. Fortunately, a good war story married to a good romance story can serve that same function without all the carnage.

So, if they do take that leap, if they do not hesitate ... are the two passionate young lovers lost? True love has presented itself, and love, in the conventional romantic sense, is not just a transcendental value but the transcendental value. Everyone in the audience suspects that, in life, there is no guarantee that "true love" will ever present itself. When it does, should not you take hold of it with both hands? Cue the violins...

If the two take the metaphoric "lovers' leap," it will probably gain some measure of initial audience approval, even though the audience is also aware that the protagonists are not entirely taking the "high road." Their choice to take the leap is, ultimately, a selfish one. The man and woman both have entanglements, commitments, and vows to keep holy. If they betray their vows, they hurt people whom they cherish. That duel cannot happen. If the Union Captain shoots the older man dead, our respect for the Captain dies too. The audience will not buy it. It will come across as murder. The story loses its audience-appeal.

No, once again, it is looking likely that if someone has to die, it has to be the young woman. If she allows the duel to happen, she will be complicit in a murder. The audience will not like that. If the Union Captain dies, we have no story. What would the story be about? "Bad things happen to good people" does not illuminate anything that we do not know. If the old man dies on his own, or kills himself, it is a different story. For the present version, there would be no reason for him to appear at all.

Storytelling cannot avoid the virtues versus vices quandary that confronts and conflicts us all. To the contrary, it is storytelling's job to wrestle with that quandary. We try to sort it out, but no matter how wise and deep we are, or think we are, we can never completely succeed at nailing the truth. Still, we must try for that is our honorable role. We must "keep on keeping on," as the venerable gospel song puts it.

The context of the Civil War gives us the hammer. Used wisely, we might just nail a little truth with it. A hammer is not a delicate instrument, but it is a powerful one. A hammer can be used to smash things to pieces or build things. War itself is a social convention that smashes conventional preconceptions of morality, especially the "thou shalt not kill" commandment. But once you open the door to the blood fest, what do you say about pillage and rape? War is full of that. It is another convention, but it is conventionally not spoken about. The Colonel is a gentleman officer leading men to war, but war is not a gentleman's pursuit. He is fully aware of the contradiction. And yet, somehow, he remains honorable within the conventional understanding. The point is that, in a way, our little wartime romance tears that convention apart with the claw-end of the hammer. This is a good thing. This is good, take-no-prisoners storytelling.

The Civil War is in the background by design. We could have chosen something else. But war serves, as it always does in storytelling, as a device to separate what we might we want to believe is true -and what we've been brought up to believe is "the good"– from what, in terms of human happiness, is really is good and true. All successful stories do a good job of addressing these questions. They shed light on them, clarify them, but do not –and cannot– offer panaceas. **The storyteller cannot provide all-encompassing solutions to the happiness question because, it seems, humans cannot. Yet, being mortal humans, storytellers must try.** We are compelled to do so by our sentience. Sentience is cognizance that we travel in a time machine towards the end of all things, towards death. That knowledge, too, is universal in the human story.

So, if we must kill off our beautiful young female protagonist, it is the situation that is at fault. It is the war. She is the only character whose death would shine a light back on the war. Her handsome young man returns to his family. The old man? Meh. He is an old man and an old plantation owner and all that implies. His world is gone and he knows it. We could allow him to live and wander like King Lear is the smoldering rubble of his world. Or not.

The above lays out the interior structure of the situation in Act II and how and why it changes from Act I. Every plot point and every characteristic has been devised to create a dynamic that gets at the story theme(s).

This means that we would need to go back and establish that for the Union Captain, there had once been "chemistry" in his relationship with his wife, but the bloom is off the rose. You know, children, the pressures of daily life? Maybe he can get some of the magic back with her. He still loves her, even if he is not in love with her anymore. He certainly feels kindness and responsibility towards her and his children. He too is a good man in a situation that forces him to wrestle with the meaning of his life. Everything is on the table in the worst way. It is a bad situation. **A bad situation in Act II is absolutely necessary if there is to be any hope of illuminating what the good situation might be.**

As for the young lady, she married a father figure –perhaps out of expediency– but he is a good man, kindly in his way, and she has grown to feel affection and admiration for him. It is just not the kind of romantic fire a young woman dreams of. Before the war, she was in an imperfect situation, but she had security, wealth, and doting kindness. You do not miss the water until the well is dry.

All of this takes place in the midst of war, which tends to turn conventional morality on its head. Our young protagonists are traumatized and badly in need of emotional release from the tension. Fate puts them together. Nature takes its course. Just as important is the deep human urge for intimacy, which provides emotional shelter from the storm. And this is one hell of a storm. The audience will stay on our lovers' side as they make passionate love in their temporary Eden. For this is war. War changes everything.

You do not always need a war, but it sure is bloody convenient. There is always some sort of storm brewing in life; the inevitably of death, for example, threatens us all. Storms of any kind provide opportunities for revelation. Every lightning bolt illuminates. And when a massive, menacing storm rolls in, we get the bonus utility of the "Who knows if they will see another sunrise?" factor. The sound of distant cannon fire is desirable here for that reason. It promotes change and gives the storyteller easy reasons for why this and that happens to the characters. **Because in a story, everything must happen for a reason.**

Maybe towards the end of Act II, the first time the lovers hear what seems to be cannon fire, it turns out to be only an approaching thunderstorm. The next time, it really is cannon fire, but carried by on a wind perfumed by the scent of sweet magnolias. Something like that. Eden must be threatened. The war needs to return to them in one form or another. The bonus is that this benefits the storyteller by reducing his or her options. And limitations are good unless you would like to take forever to finish your tale. **Do you want to write this script in two months, or two years?**

The internal logic suggests the addition of various plot devices, but these devices be kept in the background. This story remains a romance, and, as a backdrop for a romance, war is marvelous. War serves its storytelling purpose as a solvent to strip away conventional ideas and as a catalyst to explore the deeper overarching issues facing human happiness –which is what good storytelling is all about. Done right, people find that entertaining. (There will be much more on this subject in Chapter 16, "Writing to Entertain".)

Although this story exists within moral gray areas rather than the good-versus-bad of melodrama, it is worth noting that the movie version easily could be a mainstream Hollywood product. What drives any good script is themes pertinent to its target audience. This includes "art movies," "action-adventure blockbusters, " and everything in between. The commercial success of a story is not predicated on whether or not a story reinforces conventional thinking. That stated, it is equally important to understand that conventional thinking need not always be under attack.

This particular romance, cast against the backdrop of the American Civil War, creates a situation in which the story theme is amplified. That was the plan from the get-go. That stated and hopefully understood, essentially this same story, with the same basic characters and dynamics, could be set on Battlestar Galactica as science fiction, or almost anywhere, or anytime, as long as there is upheaval and intense human conflict. An earthquake could suffice. A pandemic will do. Story, characterizations, and plot can be dissected, reconstructed, and transmogrified in an infinite manner of ways and serve the same story theme(s).

What a story cannot do is NOT serve a story theme and not serve as a vehicle for understanding. Your goal is getting at what is meaningful. Meaning, therefore, is

what your Act II needs to deliver. You need to portray that meaning, and not just tell it or explain it. That really is your only job as a story-smith: to convey meaning.

It comes down to what makes life valuable, and what is worth risking for that value. There always is a risk. Peril provides the electricity for every Act II. What is the present situation now of our imaginary Act II? It is a situation wherein every choice will end up hurting someone innocent (this is also true of war). Now we are in the land where really big dragons dwell, a country in which there is no perfect anything.

Once again, the young woman must die, at least in this present situation.

But, I get it: some of you just can't abide your innocent female co-protagonist being killed off. Fine. As an exercise, let's consider an alternative twist on the tale with an alternative plot, but still going after the same story themes: What if our hero climbs back into his trousers just before crossing that line with the beautiful, young, and willing woman? What if he does not seize "true love" by the lily-white throat? What if there is no Confederate Colonel to pop out of the fog of war? Let's say the young man and the beautiful woman just part ways and we follow the man. The woman, in this version, is now demoted from co-protagonist to supporting role. Does the path of virtuousness take the Union Captain any place worth going?

Assume there is not a heavenly reward because that would be cheating (as will be made clear in a later chapter.) That assumed, how is virtue its own reward? Dealing only with what we know of this mortal coil, does our Sir Galahad earn a holy grail for his noble sacrifice? If so, what would that grail really be, aside from a trophy to go on the mantelpiece? What is the meaning of that grail? **Can you come up with an alternative Act II that gets us where we need to go? Try it.**

Having a virtuous wife and being a virtuous husband, raising virtuous children … it is just not the same as being in the throes of mad, magical, transformative love, is it? Does the choice of virtue doom the hero to an unheroic ho-hum life ever after? If so, what would be the value in telling that kind of tale? Maybe it is there somewhere. It certainly could be. One thing for certain, you as a storyteller will have to find it or abandon this approach. If you can manage to identify your theme and move on to exploit that theme, do it. The audience would now want light shed on this theme too. This could be the same audience and the same general story theme, and they could be equally captivated, via this alternate plot direction, by your storytelling mastery.

Staying on the straight and narrow, or straying from the straight and narrow, these are just plot points. Do not confuse plot with story.

Staying on the straight and narrow, doing what society expects of you, earning points from other "decent" folks; all of that coincides with conventional morality. The job of the storyteller is neither to prove nor to disprove that conventional morality is a man-made crock. Perhaps conventional morality serves a very good purpose for promoting human happiness and social well-being. Or, maybe not. You could tell a great story that supports either notion. But "making the case" is more the turf of philosophers or social scientists, than of storytellers.

That the virtuous remain virtuous is, however, a self-evident truth –and a tedious one in terms of storytelling. **If**

a truth is self-evident, why illuminate it? Leave that to medieval pageants and miracle plays. Storytelling is a dramatic art.

The opposite is equally true: Going your own way is not in itself a value. You cannot just go anywhere you want to as a professional storyteller. The audience provides the restrictions. If where you go to is repellent, and there is no pressing storytelling reason to go there, you will lose your audience. A movie like Saving Private Ryan goes to repellent places, but for very good reasons. Do not just blow things up.

Similarly, a bad person doing bad things just because he or she is bad is as uninteresting as a good person doing good things because he or she is good. If, however, something is repellent but, in a circumstance invented by the storyteller, the protagonist is forced to do it, or induced to do it, or is tricked into doing it –now we have storytelling material.

"The devil made me do it" is a blasé statement from anyone, but especially if you are a storyteller. On the other hand, if the devil makes your character do it –because your character really wants to do it anyway– then the devil is just the storyteller's helpmate, like any antagonist. Macbeth's witches serve Shakespeare in this way. With those witches, as with the Devil, it is always about choices. All we need is a trickster and a common human foible like a naughty sexual opportunity presenting itself to a wayward Jack or Jill. Then we need to discover what the consequences are for our Jack or Jill. Anything to break the tedium, right?

A theme cannot be a tautology. A theme cannot be self-evident. A pertinent story theme always needs clarification, examination, edification, and questioning. If "love is the answer," why? Why not hate? Wherever your characters stand in terms of right and wrong, you, as storyteller, are obligated to ask why this and not that. **You must satisfy the why. Meaning needs to be the outcome. If the outcome fails to satisfy your story theme, your outcome will leave your audience dissatisfied.**

5. The Climax: What It Should And Should Not Be

Act II needs to be a bumpy, risky, upward climb to the penultimate point of the story, which is called the climax.

There can be false starts and seeming dead-ends as the plot twists and turns upon itself. The audience expects to be surprised. Do not make your plot too predictable. The audience should be made to anticipate something and then fooled. Tease them. Give them just a little pinch of what they want. Then snatch most of it away. Keep them hungry in a bowl, like goldfish.

Too much is made of the hero triumphing at the climax. There is a notion that Hollywood demands the happy ending, and although mediocre Hollywood might tend that way, conflating a happy ending with entertainment is an unsupportable assumption. Hollywood, at its best, never demanded a happy ending. Many of Hollywood's biggest blockbusters do not have "Hollywood endings."

The movie *Thelma and Louise* did not end happily, at least in the conventional sense. The co-protagonists ran their car off a cliff at the climax. Many successful films are predicated on the hard truth that all too often, when almost everyone else is already corrupted, virtue earns the hero social contempt and even ignominy. Remember, if it is the truth, the audience will accept your climax, and might even applaud. The sad or cynical Hollywood ending was thematic for movies as different from each other as Batman: The Dark Knight and The Green Mile. Such stories ask the hero to sacrifice in the face of the certainty that the prospect for personal gain at the end is nil. These stories ask something deep, not just from the heroes, but also from the audience. They ask: If a hero falls in a forest with no one to see him fall, is the hero still a hero? If the heroism is widely perceived as villainy, can the audience, which is sitting in for society, accept that? Can a hero outwardly lose, yet inwardly win? Where is the measure of someone's character? In whose eyes? These kinds of tales answer that question, which really is a metaphysical question. Heroism can transcend social values and conventional morality. Heroism is not normal; it is the exception to the general rule that proves an enduring truth.

Yes, the victory at the climax of Act II can be inward only and can function as secret knowledge passed on by the storyteller to the audience or reader. A hero is a hero despite any common misperception, despite socialized ideas of right and wrong, despite whether the heroism results in almost universal shunning of the hero. Society's rules and justice can be at odds with each other, and commonly are in many of the world's greatest tales. (As we will see, the Western genre often testifies to this point of view.)

No matter how a tale is crafted, no matter how a hero fares at the climax –whether he or she is devoured by the dragon or slays it– Act II depicts HOW the protagonist manages to arrive at that penultimate point,

which can be triumph or failure –or, in more nuanced tales– it can be something in-between.

A good story starts somewhere and ends somewhere else. A good story does not go in circles. When the prodigal son returns home, he is not quite the same person, and home is not quite the same home. Some writers and teachers of storytelling call this "the hero's journey." That is a useful and credible description, but it is vital to understand that this is a journey towards at least the possibility of enlightenment. If the hero perishes at the climax unenlightened, then the death is in vain, but the hero's journey is never in vain –not from the vantage point of the audience or reader. Only if the audience also remains where they were in Act I is both the hero's journey and storytelling in vain.

Your story is meant to be a vehicle to transport your readers or audience somewhere. Shall we define "somewhere"? "Somewhere," in this context, means to some point of enlightenment. Insight, communicated through a fictional portrayal of events in which the protagonist is up against something important, is shared with the audience or reader by the story climax in every effective story. There are no exceptions. This is the only true measure of a tale well told. If the protagonist fails on that journey, that can be a justifiable plot device. Many protagonists on the journey do not end as heroes. Macbeth fails. Little Red Riding Hood is a phenomenal failure. So is Michael Corleone in Godfather II. Your success as a storyteller does not rest on the success of your protagonists by the end of Act II.

Act II consists of one or, usually a series of obstacles (tests) that the antagonist(s) places in the protagonist's path on the "hero's journey." The nature of the obstacles or tests meted out is predetermined or driven by the story theme set out in Act I. Nothing else should even appear to be predetermined. Once the climax is reached, or shortly thereafter, we are in Act III.

6. The Big Question Is, Do You Know Your Big Question?

You will need to know the Big Question that drives your tale, or your audience certainly will never know it. By all and any means, keep them guessing, keep the audience on the hook; but only to guess the answer to the Big Question. **You, the storyteller, have embedded your Big Question in Act I, so it was well established before the train got derailed by the antagonist in Act II territory. At some point, it will be on you to supply something of a Big Answer to your Big Question.**

A Big Question implies a Big Answer. In Little Red Riding Hood, the Big Question is: does this kid have the maturity and the moxie to deal with a wolf? If she keeps living in her head and playing pretend, like small children often do, she will die.

Act II is when that pursuit of the Big Answer begins. The Big Question creates the vector for your tales. This means that it governs the velocity and general direction of your plot. You do not. It does. That much should be clear by now. The propellant is your story theme. Have you identified what your tale is about? Where is your hero heading? To what pinnacle? To slay what dragon?

The Big Question is your story theme, restated as a question. Themes need to be tested; but in fiction, in the skin of a protagonist. Like any theme, yours will be elusive, and yet it will be a life-truth. It will point to the classical virtues, but through portrayal, not preaching. The virtues are connected to enduring human happiness. Happiness is a difficult pursuit. Happiness is serious business. It even took Buddha a while to figure this one out. Vice can lead to pleasure. Virtue can lead to happiness. Believe it or not.

Of course, there is no guarantee. It takes a while for mortals to gain this insight. Every theme is a slippery fish. C'est la vie. Blame nature, blame God, but for writers of fiction it is a godsend that the quest for human happiness is a difficult, often perilous journey that requires earnest, hard work of one kind or another. If it is easy to kill the dragon, your story will be meaningless.

Any insight into the Big Question that is provided through the enjoyable, irresistible, rollercoaster of a learning process we call entertainment can only be made meaningful to the audience if they have an idea of what is at stake. What is at stake needs to be a lot, and it needs to correspond with stakes familiar to your audience or reader.

But know this: There is what seems to be at stake in the plot –such as, will the two lovers be able to stay together? And there is what really is at stake, which is always some form of that most venerable of all Big Questions. Where lies human happiness? In what cave? What dragon needs to be slain to attain that holy grail?

It is happiness that is really at stake, always –but not necessarily the happiness of the protagonist. In most of the finest Westerns, the cowboy hero gets little to nothing personally from his sacrifice and heroics. All he gets is the satisfaction of knowing he did right.

Sometimes his reward includes a kick in the teeth from those he saved. Usually he ends up riding into the sunset with his only reliable friend, his horse. In many kinds of stories, others not as highly evolved as the hero reap the benefits of the sacrifice and heroics of the protagonist. These others, often called "ordinary folk," are rarely as courageous, honest, kind, forgiving, or generous as the hero.

The protagonist hero could save a person, family, or whole town, and the heroism can be without recognition within the story, never mind appreciation of those he or she saved. A story's success does not depend on appreciation from the characters within it. It depends on the recognition and appreciation of the audience. Those he saves in the story do not have to like him. They might even resent him, especially if his deeds shine a spotlight on their own hypocrisy and mendacity. The folks the hero saves can even be his enemies.

A cowboy hero has usually arrived on the scene as a stranger, and leaves the scene as a stranger. This kind of protagonist can be called a "selfless hero," meaning he has nothing directly to gain. He wins no princess. He could even lose a princess, as he almost does in High Noon. If that is the case, it prompts another Big Question: For the stories in which those saved by the deeds of the "selfless hero" remain ingrates, what makes the sacrifice valuable? Maybe he should have left them to harvest what they had sowed.

Heroes can sacrifice themselves accomplishing little to nothing substantive, but the storyteller needs to address why sacrifice in a righteous cause is good, even if no one in the tale learns a damn thing from the sacrifice. The answer is that the audience learns something about the human condition, which can be fear-driven, selfish, and stubbornly or even proudly ignorant. They learn about themselves, or an aspect of themselves. They might also learn that hope is kept alive when someone acts, even against huge odds, in a righteous cause. Maybe that sounds like preaching, so let me bring you back to the hard ground. If this is the kind of cynical tale you are driven to craft, you, the storyteller, need the above conveyed to the audience. They must get it, even if those in the story do not. **No story succeeds that does not, by the end, promote virtue.** The audience is not interested. Even Tarantino's *Reservoir Dogs* promotes virtue.

Of course, protagonists can sacrifice for a wrong cause, in which case the heroism is not heroism, but something more like foolishness. Courage on its own does not make a hero. Courage disconnected from other virtues such as compassion, generosity, and kindness cannot rise to the necessary level. Take this into account as you create your plot and decide what happens in Act II. That will simplify and limit what can happen and what cannot happen. **The more you understand what belongs and does not belong in your plot, the easier the writing will flow.**

Again, we are talking about understanding the internal logic of your story. Understanding this will liberate you and, with practice, turn you into a master storyteller. The more quickly you can answer the fundamental Big Question, "What is it about?", the better you are doing.

The general direction of your story should be clear to you from the start of the actual writing. To know where you are heading is to know your theme. Figure that out in a period we will call "storytelling pre-production." How you figure it out –whether you do research, whether you write notes, whether you interview people– that is up to you. Whatever mental or physical methodology helps you organize your thoughts and define the Big Question posed by your story theme, do it. Do it in the shower. Do it at a table in a local coffee joint, or even in a bar. Do it as you get drunk (but do not make that a habit.) Do it though. Do it before you begin to write in earnest. Do it and it will make the writing flow. It can cure a case of the dreaded "writer's block," since not knowing what you are writing about probably is the leading cause of "writer's block."

You never start your story-train in the direction of your actual story in Act I. You begin by seeming to be going somewhere and then, et voila, something happens and you are heading somewhere else. **Act I is about who, what, when, where, and what seems to be the situation and setting. Seems is what is operative in Act I. Act I is also where you must embed the theme.**

The starting situation in Act I is where you lay out the Big Question. The audience does not have to know what the Big Question is. At least, they do not need to be able to articulate it. They just need to intuit it, to feel it. As the storyteller, however, you need to be able to articulate it, if only to yourself. This is mandatory since your job will be to address the Big Questions of life and clarify life's big themes, not as a philosopher but by means of portrayal. Do not lecture.

You need to focus the incoherent scattered light into a coherent beam. Just at the right moment, you, through the agency of your antagonist, will switch the story-train to the real direction that it needs to go, which is always towards illumination. **This happens at the end of Act I, and is where Act II opens –now heading in a different direction. Always.**

Your story theme creates your story content, and you are but the agent of a process. A storyteller is an alchemist, transmuting something base into something extraordinary and precious. As such, you should be aware of what particular base content of life you are going to transmute upward in this particular tale. **What is your Big Question? How are you going to supply the Big Answer?**

For example, the Big Question driving The Godfather II is: How does an intelligent, well-meaning human being lose his or her moral compass? The process of corruption defeating the better angels of the central protagonist, Michael Corleone, is brilliantly depicted in Act II of that film. In Act I, however, young, clever, dashing Michael Corleone is introduced as someone contemptuous of the family business and determined to lead a moral and normal life. That is made crystal clear.

Also in Act I, we are given insight into what young Michael is up against. We are supplied with something concrete, something that connects with our emotions. It is not just an ideal presented here. Michael will need to turn his back on his family, where life is depicted as appealingly warm, supportive, friendly, loving, and seemingly normal. Ultimately, this might be an illusion. If so, it is a meaningful illusion to Michael Corleone, and it would be meaningful to you as well. In other words, the stakes are real for him, and they are made real for the audience. If Michael turns his back on the family business, he also turns his back on all the good that comes with it. And so, it appears in Act I that idealistic Michael Corleone has a surplus of what we all want to have: wealth, love, good looks, intelligence, poise, and a loving support system. And yet …

Do not be fooled: even if the Big Question is apparent to you, it rarely will be to the audience, without you, the teller of the tale, making it clear. You need to make it apparent in the set-up in Act I that, if it had been you, dear reader or audience member, in a similar situation you would feel the same way as the protagonist does. This is necessary to achieve "audience buy-in."

There can be no doubt that, had the audience been born into the situation Michael Corleone finds himself in Act I, they would act and feel much the way he does. Nevertheless, this is a stretch. These are very bad people, who do terrible, violent things in the name of profit. We are made to buy into his situation, and his dilemma, not by happy accident but through the storytelling craft of the writers and director of this film. Michael Corleone's literal dilemma is unlikely to directly correspond to what anyone in the audience faces, but neither would Hamlet's. This, then, is a plot device that serves as a metaphor. What counts is that the metaphor connects with the lives of your audience members, whose lives are hopefully not quite this dramatic.

The important thing to note is that in Act I, the audience is charmed by what seems to be an old fashioned happy, warm family; but they are repelled, and to a degree confused, by the reality of what the family does to maintain that illusion. Thanks to some good writing and great directing, they have been put in Michael Corlone's fancy Italian shoes.

Few in the audience are likely to have been born into a mafia don's family, but the situation is not dissimilar from remaining loyal to and supportive of your country, even as it does things you find morally repugnant. All good fiction is metaphor. Francis Ford Coppola was shooting The Godfather Part II when the Vietnam War was at its most unpopular. For me, the genius of this, the greatest of all mob movie sequels, is that the mafia serves as a stage for depicting the greater theme about the seductive power of corruption, an issue that confronts all of us. Francis Ford Coppola is a good Catholic boy; he demonstrated through these films his genuine concern about the soul of America. The mafia serves as but a means to that end.

Not many people are likely to read the moral philosophers on this Big Question; but put a human skin on it, tell a good story, and you can spare your audience the trouble of plowing through Aristotle, Thomas Aquinas, or Immanuel Kant. You can even have a blockbuster hit. (Of course, "blockbuster" does not always equate with "deep" –in fact, usually the opposite is the case. But not here.)

The Corleone family is rich, powerful, and most importantly, widely respected by hard-working, solid people in their community, despite those same "ordinary folk" knowing about the family's corrupt and violent methods. Clearly, there are many practical advantages to being Michael Corleone, the son of an admired don. The audience knows it will not be easy for him to turn his back on what fortune has given him as a birthright. If they are honest with themselves, they will know that if they were in Michael Corleone's position, it would not be easy for them, either. This is solidly laid down as the foundation for the story in Act I. The audience is now significantly aware of the story theme. What is at stake here is not just the soul of one idealistic young man, but by extension, the soul of one young idealistic nation as well. That too is implicit in Act I of The Godfather II, but not by accident –it has been made implicit.

The universal theme of the tale can be expressed in Biblical terms: "What profit a man if he gains the world, but loses his soul?" (Mark 8:6). What specifically does Michael Corleone lose and what does he gain? Because his is the skin this theme is wrapped in, he definitely gains and he definitely loses. What is the true worth of profit reaped from vice? What does he lose of value as he chooses vice over virtue? Because he definitely chooses. Does it matter in the end if he valiantly struggled against his destiny? Or was it destiny? Or is this outcome the consequence of poor choices? There are many things to learn as we accompany Michael Corleone on his downward spiral through Act II.

Act II makes it clear what almost superhuman strength of character Michael Corleone would have had to possess to be able to maintain his virtue when, clearly, maintaining virtue means losing profound material advantages, as well as being shunned by the family he cannot help loving.

So here, in a movie full of violence, coarseness, and carnality, we must grapple with a metaphysical issue, posed here as a Big Question: what is, in fact, real and important? Money? Power? What is worth giving up to remain virtuous? What gains a man? This is necessarily a metaphysical question or, if you prefer, a spiritual issue, since in a purely animal sense, Michael Corleone choosing to accept and exploit his advantages makes sense.

Now, grounded in a spiritual versus material dichotomy, the audience is primed for an exciting Act II –which they get in spades. This story is a tragedy told on an almost operatic scale. We watch Michael Corleone morally succumb incrementally, as we incrementally lose our sympathy for him; yet even by the end of Act II, we have not entirely given up on him.

Mario Puzo and Francis Ford Coppola, the co-writers of this Oscar-winning movie, understood that it was necessary to clearly stipulate the stakes for Michael Corleone in Act I. So they put human flesh on what is at stake. They created a woman, beautiful and wholesome. She is where Michael would like to be. She represents the holy grail. They pitted his love of this good woman, and the authentic family values Michael and his young wife wanted to co-create, against The Family values.

I cannot think of any movie that has a more riveting and poignant climax: a wonderfully intercut scene where, in a gorgeous church, Michael Corleone and his wife attend their first son's baptism while, in juxtaposition, his henchmen, at that very moment, are carrying out his orders to bloodily massacre the rival gangsters. **This is both Michael's first brilliant coup as a gangster boss and also, the moment of his fall from grace. He is now a failure as a human being. We are nearly at the end of Act II.**

It is not difficult to tie up such a brilliantly realized Act II with a bow. Act III leaves Michael Corleone as an empty vessel. He is a failure in his wife's eyes, his own eyes, and the audience's eyes. He is profoundly alienated and alone. He has lost everything of true value, even as he has made exponential gains in the material world.

But there is something else about this movie that propels it way beyond mere entertainment. While it is tragic that a person, full of hope and potential in Act I, has become as corrupt, hypocritical, and violent as his father, his failure to rise morally is relatable given that he operates in a hyper-corrupt, poisonous world. He has been defeated in an environment in which rising above the miasma of corruption and duplicity would seem to require superhuman strength of character. Michael Corleone is no ordinary man, but he is not superhuman. That was made clear in Act I. He is gifted, charming, sincere, and extraordinarily likable, with a passionate desire to do what is right. His fall from grace is the fall of a hero. The point is that Michael Corleone is not just like us. He is actually better than most of us. And yet even he succumbs to evil, as do we in so many ways, individually, as a civilization, or even as a species.

This movie takes on, and takes on grimly, a Big Question about who we are, as opposed to who we need to be. Francis Ford Coppola makes Michael Corleone's downfall our downfall, collectively and personally. If Michael is to be condemned, so are we all; that is the summation of Act III.

7. Decisions, Decisions

The outcome of your tale –meaning if your protagonists will live happily ever after or not– needs to be kept uncertain, and a positive ending kept doubtful from early on. This means at the end of Act I, and throughout Act II until the climax, you need to keep the audience hoping for the best, but expecting the worst. Act II is when the protagonist earns a positive outcome, or falls short.

The function of Act III is to supply the answer to that happy ending question. Just announcing that the protagonists did or did not make the grade in the summation, however, is not enough. There are rules: the audience needs a sense of WHY that is the outcome, and not some other. The outcome will have to be the logical result of decisions that the antagonists forced the protagonists to make in Act II, or it will not satisfy. If the audience does not appreciate the logic, they will feel cheated. They will be let down. **At core, Act II assesses the character mettle of the hero/protagonist. Act III presents the certificate.**

Little Red is devoured by a wolf, not just because there happen to be wolves in the woods, but because she is an immature twit who fails to pay attention to potential hazards in her path. Silly girl, she makes stupid choices, and just about everyone in the target demographic understands why she gets what she gets. The audience appreciates this, and is satisfied by the end of the tale. And if you require an afterword, that afterword might be: Burp.

A protagonist triumphs over what is placed in his or her way because he or she possesses the right traits –courage, kindness, generosity, humility, insight, cleverness, awareness, patience– whatever goes into making the right decisions and carrying them out.

The Wolf does not beat Little Red: Little Red beats Little Red. She failed to appreciate what a wolf is and what the woods are. She failed to understand who was in that bed. She asked some very stupid questions. She became lunch. Little Red Riding Hood is an instructional fable. If you are going to venture into the woods, know the woods.

You can perish at the hand of an antagonist, but that is not what damns you. Naiveté is what damned Little Red. The decisions that emerge out of the fiber of character is what redeems or damns a protagonist. A wolf is just a type of dragon, metaphorically speaking. All stories feature some kind of dragon. In a sense, all dragons are just doing their jobs. If a righteous protagonist falls victim to a dragon, that is the essence of a Shakespearian tragedy. So be it. *Romeo and Julliet* is just such a tragedy. The dragon in that tale is the moral laxity of the society in which they lived. Kick it up a level and you can generalize: the fallen state of man destroys all Edens. Shakespeare liked to kick it up a level.

This is why dumb luck cannot come into it. Dumb luck bypasses all that is important in storytelling. Red's wolf cannot be struck dead by a lightning bolt to end Act II in Red's favor. Red must outsmart the Wolf or fail to, and in this case, she fails to. That is on her and the boys and girls watching the cartoon or reading the book know the onus is on the Little Red. The instruction embedded in this instructional fable, however, is that the onus is also on them. Know the woods.

In reality, pit a healthy wolf against a six year old, and I would put odds on the wolf. He would be the winner by what might be called evolutionary good fortune. But in the tale, if the Wolf simply falls upon Little Red and devours her just because he can, that would not make for an interesting story. It is not just that this is too predictable; it fails even the definition of a story. It would be just an incident, another bad thing that happens to another good person. No revelation there because there was no test of virtue, acumen, and ability there. You absolutely need Red's three dumb questions –you know the ones, about big ears, big eyes and especially those massive canines– to make this story work for its target demographic, little children. This constitutes the climax of Act II and clearly places the onus on Little Red. Little Red Riding Hood is, thus, a tragedy, like Macbeth.

This is the same reason you need to keep God and luck out of your scripts –in the sense of the agency that determines a story's outcome. (There will be a lot more on this in the next chapter.) **The agency that leads to the story's outcome has to remain with the protagonist. (Not the antagonist.)** Whether that agency leads to a good or bad outcome for the protagonist is immaterial. The protagonist may go down in a blaze of glory. In that case, the blaze of glory is what illuminates. No one can give anyone glory, not even the good Lord. Glory is earned. Anything else renders that protagonist's character-arc moot. No character-arc, no story worth reading or watching.

If, as in Macbeth or Little Red Riding Hood, the protagonists do not earn the glory, and in fact earn the opposite, the audience needs to be clear on what character flaws led to the tragic ending. The witches of Macbeth, and the Wolf in Little Red Riding Hood, only prompt the protagonist to make choices.

This is from the original storybook:

"He asked her where she was going. The poor child, not knowing that it was dangerous to stop and listen to a wolf, said: 'I am going to see my grandmother, and I am taking her a cake and a pot of butter which my mother has sent to her.'" "Does she live far away?" asked the Wolf."

Clearly there are any number of answers that could have put the wolf off his game here. Little Red chooses to reply candidly. The choices a protagonist makes reveal the mettle of his or her character.

Every four-year-old can see that it is a wolf, not Granny, in the bed. Little Red could have chosen the evidence

155

before her and, at least, tried to run away. If she got away, though, there would have to be a damn good reason, and the reason would have to be that Red had the smarts, the gumption, and the prowess to escape the slobbery jaws of the Wolf.

The same stipulations apply to happy endings. The "happy ending" of Act III of Star Wars IV, which is that they live to fight another day, was the result of the aggregate virtues of the intergalactic heroes –virtues not just claimed, but proven in Act II. Included as a virtue was their faith in The Force. This is similar to faith in God, but it is clear they had to choose to put their faith in this higher power and finding that faith was not easy. After that, they need training to harness The Force. It was always on them.

Simply put, antagonists do not defeat protagonists so much as protagonists defeat themselves. When protagonists make the right choices and end up nevertheless losing, that serves to ennoble their character-arcs. Heroes can be vanquished, or perish, and yet remain stellar examples of virtue for the rest of us.

8. Keeping Faith And The Good Lord Out Of Your Storytelling

Your life might be based on faith. Your story cannot be. You cannot satisfy the question "why" with "because The Lord says so." Whether God is personally in your life or not, He cannot be the reason why things turn out the way they do in a story. God or the gods can have a role in your story, like any characters; but any divine act, such as, for example, a lightning bolt conveniently striking your villain dead at the end of Act II, renders your protagonist's journey worthless. **Characters must make choices, and characters must face the consequences. Faith, therefore, must be like any other character trait of a protagonist, and it too needs testing.**

If belief or faith is all it takes for humans to reach the promised land, there would be no need to tell any of the instructional tales and parables that populate the written mission statements of all the great faiths, from the Bhagavad Gita to the Bible. Stories are vehicles of meaning, which is why the great books of faith rely on storytelling.

To paraphrase Yoda, The Force may be with you, but training to do good with the Force, you must have.

Any story that answers the question "Why?" with "Because the Bible tells us so" is not a story. Actually, even the Bible does not tend to do that much; it provides reasons why. And anyway, it is too late for God to intervene. Eve and Adam took that away from us. They tasted the forbidden fruit from the Tree of Knowledge. Ever since, the onus has been on us.

Like Adam and Eve, their descendants (to stick with the metaphor) will also want a taste from the Tree of Knowledge. If, as in Genesis, God created man and woman, it was Adam and Eve who gave birth to storytelling. If, like Moses, your protagonist fails to enter the "Promised Land," your audience still needs to arrive there –in the sense that every teller of tales makes a promise to transport the audience to the apex of a proverbial mountain.

In Act I, you hint that there is a Promised Land –which you do in the form of embedding a theme. In Act II, you show the way to the promised land. It matters not if your protagonist is a hero who falls short like Moses, or if something truly great is achieved as Frodo manages to do in The Lord of The Rings. What matters is that light is shed on the Big Questions of life, and that, whatever the ending in Act III, it is the earned result of the protagonist's exercise of free will.

God cannot guide anyone's hand. God can only give sound advice. So can a grandmother. Choices need to be made under challenging circumstances in every Act II. These choices are offered by an antagonist. That antagonist is your avatar (you, the storyteller). You, in effect, are offering challenges to test the mettle of your protagonist's character, which when acted upon will simultaneously illuminate your story theme(s).

God references aside, what I am really saying is that any outcome that results from any agency other than that of your protagonist's acumen and ability, at the very least, will weaken your tale. That includes the agency called "blind luck."

Storytellers face their own dragon as they write every Act II of every story, novel, or screenplay. The dragon is unavoidable. Take courage. Keep your wits about you. Respect, even love, your dragon, but do not be fooled. A dragon is a dragon. A wolf is a wolf.

9. Drama, Melodrama

Melodrama: A sensational dramatic piece with exaggerated characters and exciting events intended to appeal to the emotions.

Every story, including melodramas, concerns at least one Jack slaying at least one dragon, or one Jack not being up to the task. What constitutes a "dragon" is anything standing in the way of well-being and happiness.

Happiness is for the protagonists to gain or lose, but you, the storyteller, also need to build a bridge to the audience's inherent desire for their own well-being and happiness. Your story must intersect with their interests, hopes, and fears. Any story, in a nutshell, is one or more protagonists undertaking a journey-quest and gaining some degree of happiness by Act III; or failing to do so. You do not necessarily need a "happily-ever-after" "Hollywood ending" but by Act III you must have proven your case. You do this through portrayal, not in essay form. Do your job and it will resonate with the happiness question. Because the audience has been wondering about that, often obsessively. They may not know it, but this is really why they paid the price of admission.

It is not the act of slaying the dragon, so much as it is the quest, that is the gist of storytelling. Not coincidentally, this also seems to be how it works for the attainment of human happiness. It is on the way to our Act III that we find ourselves, or not.

Melodramas do not seriously address these issues, or at best, just gloss over them, handing out pat answers to life's Big Questions like prizes in Cracker

159

Jack boxes. There is little to no addressing "why" in melodrama.

A writer of dramatic fiction, as opposed to those who hack out melodramas, must address the big whys of life. They must know how to invest a sense of the universal into their protagonist's journey. Little Red Riding Hood may not be written on the grand scale of Tolstoy's War And Peace, but this perfect little tale matters to small children who, naturally enough, do not want to be eaten by wolves. Every few years comes a new crop of them who are made cognizant, through the storyteller's craft, of something higher, and that did not just happen by accident. Mostly through the device of three dumb questions, it is clear to the young audience, if not to the twit, that these questions are being asked of what is definitely not a granny. It is a wolf! The little kiddies make the leap from the specifics of the tale to its universal theme because of the tragic outcome. They understand why it had to be this outcome. They are brought to the understanding that if you are too naive, you are in grave danger of tragedy befalling you. It is very sad. The woods seemed so nice. It is a harsh lesson to internalize.

This is not melodrama. This is actual drama. The story takes kiddies by the hand and leads them on a journey in which they become aware that they must grow up and learn how to face a tough, often hostile world; Mama will not necessarily be here to protect them. A precondition needed to make an unpleasant outcome unlikely, when dealing with wolves, is to first internalize the fact of wolves, and then learn how to avoid being their lunch. When that happens, we call it cognition, which is a kind of connecting the dots that happens in the brain.

For any Jack to slay any dragon, the feat must involve more than just courage and brawn. Both qualities belong to many animals, and many animals have more of both than most humans. To be an effective tale for a human audience, the action in Act II needs to also involve brain triumphing over brawn. In many confrontations, possessing a big brain is our one big advantage.

Early humans were not the strongest or fastest beasts on the savanna. They were, however, the brainiest. Brain over brawn is central to the human condition. Brain, in this sense, is not just the aptitude for abstract reasoning, but also the ability to creatively reverse engineer and apply general principles to solve practical problems. An example of a practical problem for our early ancestors might be, how can a puny human turn a huge mastodon into lunch?

Brain is also the source of our intuition, compassion, and emotional intelligence, all of which combine uniquely within each of us. Sometimes we refer to that sort of brain as "heart." In the story of Adam and Eve, Eve eats of the Tree of Knowledge. After biting into the enticing fruit, Adam and Eve develop a rash of itchy awareness.

Humans are in possession of a body that is doomed to fail them. Adam and Eve become aware that they are not just bodies, but that the body is how they get along. Thus, there is in this particular tale an awkward moment for the first two humans in which "They knew that they were naked and were ashamed." Tout de suite, Adam and Eve are no longer innocent like the other animals or like small children. The human self, in this altered state, becomes separated from the body, and out of the schism, the concept "mind" is born of brain.

A binary universe is also born. Adam and Eve are now required to choose between good and evil. This is not always that easy. The Biblical tale goes on at length to portray just how difficult it is to choose virtue over vice. In Exodus, the Lord finally hands out rules carved into stone, and it still isn't all that easy for "His children" to choose right from wrong –which all makes for excellent drama.

This is the human drama: Adam and Eve become aware of birth and death. It is the humdinger of all dilemmas. Cognizance first occurs in Act I of The Bible, or Genesis. This is where the human journey changes tracks and Act II begins. Adam and Eve are hoofed out of the Garden of Eden, and into the wilderness, which is another way of saying that they are tossed out of the known and into the unknown.

In Genesis, both the benefits and costs of sentience, which is another word for this altered state, are triggered in our mythic antecedents. Myth or not, the story of Adam and Eve offers insight into the human condition, even as it poses more questions than answers. Metaphysics aside, whether or not you are religious, this is a cracking good tale worth ruminating over.

After the exile from God's candy store, humans become sucked into an internal struggle in which their better angels wrestle with their demons. This struggle between our personal angels and demons is a life-long sentence. If you are a Buddhist, you do not buy into this as, necessarily, a life-long struggle. You can step off "the wheel of fire." If you are a Catholic, the only way out is to go to heaven. (Saint Peter has the keys.) **How you get back to the garden is the point of all religions, and, not coincidentally, also of all storytelling.** No one said it is easy. (Except for maybe Fundamentalist evangelists.) It should not seem to be easy in your story either. Slaying the dragon is a mighty task. It requires virtue and, again, the kind of smarts poor Little Red Riding Hood lacked.

If you are a storyteller, the struggle to regain Eden is fodder for your cannon, and if you are prolific, also fodder for your canon.

If you are Plato, the analogy for who we are is a demon chained to an angel. As he would have it, the tension between the inner angel and the inner demon powers the human journey. The most important aspect of Plato's analogy is neither the demon nor the angel alone, but the chain that binds them to each other.

The tension on Plato's chain, and the violent shock to our well-being and happiness as the chain snaps back and forth in the interior battle, constitutes rich storytelling ore to mine and smelt into something that shines light on the meaning of this struggle.

The struggle wears on us, and can sap our happiness. This is the process that Sigmund Freud called "neurosis." He argued, somewhat fatalistically, that neurosis is the price we pay for living within a civilization and gaining its benefits, which might include security and the opportunity to enjoy a fine Austrian wienerschnitzel or a Mozart opera. His investigations into the minds of his patients, which he referred to as their psyches, were intended to discover ways of mitigating his patient's neurosis. Storytelling is another way.

As with storytelling, the job for Dr. Freud was to shine light on the gurgling, bubbling subconscious, and coax out the engines of our unhappiness from the murky mess. For a Freudian, neurosis can be mitigated, but

163

never entirely destroyed. Other cultures, especially in the East, suggest there is a way off that wheel of fire; but Freud, a splendid neurotic himself, was nothing if not a Westerner.

The methodology for Freud that is supposed to lead a neurotic towards greater well-being and happiness is the process he called psychoanalysis. Psychoanalysis leads to self-awareness, or is at least supposed to. Self-awareness leads to a greater portion of happiness, or is at least supposed to. There are plenty of arguments about this contention as a practical matter amongst various schools of psychologists. Whatever. What is salient here for spinners of tales is that this is very much like what happens during the process of storytelling.

The aim of every good story is to shed illumination on meaning. This is also how every tale is a morality tale –a term which has had a bad reputation because it is confused with the term "melodrama."

We do not ask morality of a dog, and neither did Doctor Freud. We ask it of a human because, without it, we tear each other apart –unlike dogs, who usually manage to sort themselves out. **Morality works its way into every good tale because the human condition is one in which we have to choose between virtue and vice. This ability is known as free will.** Without at least the assumption of free will, no storytelling is possible.

Morality is at issue in every good tale, but much of what is commonly referred to as "morality" is really cultural beliefs or social norms –such as at what age someone should be allowed to marry, and to whom. For storytelling, however, social acceptability is not the main issue. In many tales, social acceptability is at odds with virtue. (To Kill A Mockingbird is an excellent example.) Social acceptability varies between societies and cannot be made into universal themes. The attempt, though, is frequently apparent in poor writing, and, of course, always in melodrama, which cannot but help to be grounded in the conventional. **Better writers explore through their art what promotes human happiness and what does not –regardless of social norms. This is a considerably more difficult, daring, and, I would add, more interesting way to write and is the main reason why drama trumps melodrama.**

10. Exploring Universal Themes As Entertainment

A Little About Writing the Great Romance

In my opinion, the much argued "serious writers" versus "writers who just want to entertain" dichotomy is a crock. Stories explore the human condition and define what brings value and happiness to the human journey. There is no end-run around this. Whatever entertainment may mean to you personally, whether it is Equus, Caddie Shack, Bugs Bunny or Macbeth, fiction is a means to get at meaning.

Alfred Hitchcock once said, "Film your murders like love scenes, and film your love scenes like murders." What can be more entertaining than a sexy boy/girl romance —except perhaps, a nice little murder? But leaving the crime, war, and thriller genres aside for the moment, consider the genre, romance. An important truth: Winning a princess or prince, as those married to one will often testify, does not automatically open the gate to the magic kingdom where "they lived happily ever after." We

165

often become disenchanted once the bloom is off the rose. The Cole Porter lyric says it better:

If we'd thought of it, 'bout the end of it,
when we started painting the town,
We'd have been aware that our love affair
was too hot not to cool down.

This too seems to be the human condition: To become enchanted and then become disenchanted seems to be almost inevitable. And yet, stepping from a marvelous illusion into the cold light of reality can feel like being thrown under a bus. Many stories follow this as a general plot. Often it seems that we crave the experience of disenchantment as much as enchantment. Is it our angels at war with our demons? Why? Why bring the romantic house of cards down on us? There is your basic romance story right here. Then he finds out about her lover ...

As the great Psalm puts it in Ecclesiastes 3:1, "For everything there is a season." Romantic relationships tend to be subject to the rule of seasons, going from spring to winter, as in Joni Mitchell's *Circle Game*:

And the seasons they go round and round
And the painted ponies go up and down
We're captive on the carousel of time
We can't return we can only look
Behind from where we came
And go round and round and round
In the circle game

In a romantic relationship, at issue is what is lasting and fulfilling after the bloom is off the rose. In real life, as in a story, the sex mostly functions as glue. But what is the glue really holding together? It does not take two people long to figure out that pleasure does not equate to happiness. You have a guaranteed audience for a romance because there is compelling interest in the subject. Whatever romance is, most of us seem to want to be put under its spell. There is compelling interest in spinning the straw of pleasure into the gold of happiness. There is compelling interest in the esoteric mysteries of Eros. Many women seem endlessly fascinated by this genre. But romance is also interesting to males, provided the presentation is not soapy or gauzy melodrama.

When love goes sour, we might seek a therapist for guidance and, hopefully, answers; but in a movie, or a novel, we do not expect answers. We expect insight, which is different. It seems that for humans, as opposed to, say, fruit flies, love is complex, mystifying, bewildering, and always a life-changing event. Romance, or whatever you want to name the situation when the animal/sexual is tethered to the ethereal/spiritual, is very important to us. This is a theme-rich genre.

Remember Plato? When it is about connecting body to spirit, focus on the connection. Focus on what chains the two together. The chain is there, whether the characters are aware of it or not. Romance is but one way of getting at the same old, eternally renewable human quandary, and the goal is what it always is: to find what is meaningful and lasting –in this genre and/or within a relationship.

Shakespeare writes with equal adroitness about war, murder, and romance. You can as well.

When something as powerful as falling in love occurs, profound issues bubble to the surface. The love of your life deciding that you are not the love of his or her life –or

167

you pulling the plug– raises deep existential questions that stare you in the face. No matter how hard you have worked to dodge these questions, after one of these experiences, it is almost impossible to dodge them any longer.

It seems that the need to confront deep questions is written into our DNA. How else to explain its endurance in all times, cultures and historic époques of storytelling? Life's nagging questions nag on, usually below the surface; but in love or war, they rise like Captain Ahab's great white whale. A story simply fetches metaphysical issues to the surface in an agreeable way. At bottom are the great human mysteries, such as: do we transcend selfishness?

Here lurk profundities that even a mainstream audience is keen on exploring. They just may not know it yet. If it seems almost definitive of the mainstream –that they tend to be only distantly aware of their true motivations to read a book, or go to a movie– it does not matter. There is no need to chide them for that. Use it to your advantage. Portraying romantic relationships –the possible traps, the differing proclivities of males and females, the shared difficulties and rewards, the expectations and the realities– any way you write the love story, if you do it well, hones in on ground-zero for human happiness. They are interested.

Merely mentioning some of the most entertaining romance flicks made in the Fifties, such as Breakfast at Tiffany's, Pillow Talk, Some Like It Hot and The Apartment, can bring smiles to people from that generation. That mainstream audience is very old now, but the romantic comedies of the era are often brilliant, funny, marvelously executed, and as worth watching today as when they were released.

All these classic romantic comedies take on big ideas, but not in the abstract. Big ideas are present, but indirectly stated. Instead, the story themes are clothed in attractive human flesh and in witty, insightful dialogue. Beneath the banter, innuendos, and teasing (it was almost all foreplay in those days), there is profound exploration. These are movies that move the audience not despite being entertainment, but because they are entertainment. **It is entertainment when big ideas are made enjoyable and accessible to the audience or readership.**

Many romance scripts portray how love relationships tend to either evolve or devolve over time. They sort out what factors and characteristics of the protagonists might make one relationship work out, while another fails. In life, the giddy Act I of falling in love almost always seems to fade to an Act II that tests the bond between the lovers. These tales pose this question: If we stay true to the person we are in a relationship with, even after the bloom is off the rose, what are we giving up? What are we gaining? (For an excellent exploration of this theme, see The Seven Year Itch.)

Other romantic fiction takes on another infinitely recyclable issue: Is it possible to change the character of someone with whom you are in love? (See The Taming of The Shrew.)

Here are some other Big Questions that romantic flicks often take on: Do you have to pay for emotional highs and carnal pleasure with agony and soul suffering? Do we always leave pieces of ourselves and our lovers on the battlefield of romance gone sour? As the song puts it, "Love hurts." Why? Is love worth the price of admission? Almost everyone reaches a point of exhaustion in a relationship when they ask themselves, "Why not just take my fill of pleasure and move on?" No answer completely satisfies. Cynicism tends to ring hollow. One-night-stands seem to be but a phase. They rarely satisfy. Most people dust themselves off and return to the pursuit of love. Yet love has been described both as a disease and a compulsion. There is so much for the storyteller to bring light to, if she or he dares to bite the apple.

Thousands of books, movies, and plays –and way too many country songs– are fashioned from such raw clay. As alluded to in a toast from the TV series Battlestar Galactica, "Here's to marriage. That's why they build bars."

In a story, if not always in life, there comes the penultimate climax at the end of Act II. Then comes a conclusion, the "summing up" in Act III. Unlike life (excepting for the fact of death) a story has to have some sort of closure that makes sense to the audience. Life does not often provide that, but stories must. Even the lovers finally settling for each other, bumps and all, can suffice as an ending, if it is earned. Compromise and acceptance can be acts of love.

Then there is the opposite kind of romantic ending, the uncompromising variety, epitomized by the "convertible driven over a cliff" climax. That ending did very well at the box office for the film, Thelma and Louise.

Especially these days, a conventional, "they were married, had healthy children, and lived happily-ever-after" conclusion is more common in Hollywood than in real life. This ending only works in a story if you can prove the case. Again, as the storyteller, you are duty bound to provide a "why," not just a "how." Why did those two manage to make it work, when so many others do not?

A romantic story, like any tale, is an attempt to get at nothing less than meaning, whether the romance is _Jane Eyre, It Happened One Night_, or _Pretty Girl_. Romances, in particular, test the possibility of losing oneself in something more marvelous than oneself, what someone once called "the blissful act of self-forgetting." This can suffice as a metaphor for the act of sex as well. That the sex act is a metaphor is basic for almost all romantic fiction, books and movies.

The object of love is poetically referred to as the beloved. The beloved does not have to be a human. It could be music (Amadeus) or mathematics (Eternal Sunshine of The Spotless Mind), for example. What makes it romantic is what the eccentric English Edwardian writer F. R. Rolfe called "the desire and pursuit of the whole."

A romance is an attempt at reaching a state of wholeness in which the lovers are two parts of one whole. Or at least, try to be.

11. Separating The Wheat From The Chaff

Ribald and Naughty Bits

Writing fiction is a process in which you separate the wheat of what really matters, from the chaff of what really does not matter.

If your protagonist gets sloshed one night and ends up in a strange bed with a stranger, you might choose to portray the scene graphically, or not. Which way to go is the question. What is not terribly pertinent to the answer is your sense of sexual boundaries or the audience's sense of decency. The issue is, what works –what works to further meaning and what conveys that meaning to the audience. If graphic sex helps that along, I would say go for it. If it does not, restrain yourself. It is always the understanding of the internal poetic logic of the yarn you are spinning that should guide your hand.

Choosing to shy away from the naughty bits or graphically portray them is a question of storytelling utility. Will you reveal more meaning via explicit portrayal of sex or violence? That should be your overriding consideration.

If your explicit lovemaking scene, or graphic portrayal of chopping off a head, does not serve to shed light on the Holy Grail of your quest –meaning– then it is gratuitous and will weaken your tale. You need to be brutally honest with yourself about that. Anything unnecessary does your tale harm.

If you do retain the naughty bit, know that what is more important in a story is not the lurid moment, or any kind of moment, but what happens before and after that moment.

Let us say your characters have sex in this plot point. Then what? A night of physical debauchery may be relatively inconsequential to the characters, which might be what you need to demonstrate; or it may be a game-changer. Whatever it is, it needs to bear its own weight and connect to other plot points on your story spine. All plot points and all scenes need to be the opposite of gratuitous. They need to add to your story. Avoid a gratuitous word.

An inconsequential sex or violence scene will end up being inconsequential for your audience, even if graphic portrayal had temporarily glued the audience's attention to the screen. If empty sex or violence leads to the realization, for your character, that this is not the road to fulfillment, then that too needs to be made clear. If it is made clear, that would then justify its inclusion. But do not try to make anything clear that does not align with the story theme(s). You would only be spinning your wheels. If it does not belong, toss it. Again, for the storytelling magi, it is a question of utility, not morality.

If Lover "A," after a one night stand, falls head-over-heels in love with Lover "B," but Lover "B" fails to hear the celestial music and that speaks to your story theme, make it as cogent and compelling a scene as you possibly can. If explicit portrayal helps, do that. If not, do not be so explicit. **Remember, you have the freedom to choose what the consequence is of any event in your story, but not the freedom to choose how the audience will react to it. Whatever makes the story stronger and more meaningful is not gratuitous.**

12. The Plot Thickens – And Then What?

When fishing for trout, you may find that finesse is needed to get them to take the bait. Reel them in, fool them and let them reel it out, bring them in patiently and deliberately until you have the fish in your net. Let the fish learn just who is in control. You are seeking nothing less than to gain dominion over minds. You do that, though, keeping in your own mind that however you play a scene, once it is over, it is in the past for the audience. **This is why, after each and every scene, you want the** audience asking, "And then what?" That is how you keep them hooked.

Once on the hook, a storyteller is duty-bound to supply the audience with a credible answer to "And then what?", but rarely immediately after the question is posed. You want to do that at a propitious moment down the road … and probably also up a mountain, through foreboding woods and into a cave, wherein dwells a dragon. On that journey, no event (scene) should entirely satisfy. Quite the contrary. It is best that it does not. Keep playing that game until the climax. If the pay-off for an "And then what?" question posed on the road up the mountain triggers yet another, but deeper question, you are doing the job right. That is called "thickening the plot."

By all and any means, thicken the plot when you can and, if you can manage it, do not supply a pay-off that the audience expects. Hint at an "either this or that," and then deliver a third option. Keep them off balance. Play bait and switch, but never cheat by giving them something that entirely fails to satisfy an "And then what?" you had posed earlier on the journey.

Forget the trout. Consider the goldfish. Give them just a nibble. Give them just enough. As with goldfish, do not overfeed and do not underfeed. Leave the audience a little hungry at the end of every scene, until the climax.

The climax is different. It must entirely satisfy.

13. Pacing

Advice commonly given is to get the audience into a scene a little late and get them out a little early. This is good advice. Do not overwrite.

The audience will want to see where you are heading with any scene, but you can play them on the hook for a while. Then, at just the right moment, after you have played them just long enough, give them another hint of where this tale is heading, another tug on the line. Every good writer plays the fish differently, but every good writer eventually reels the fish in. Timing is the issue. If you pay off a scene too early, the pay-off will be in danger of not being meaningful to the audience. If it comes too late, they have already mentally drifted off. You have thrown away an "aha" moment.

You need to establish a rhythm. Then you have to break that rhythm. **Storytelling is a process of revelation, and if you reveal too much too soon, curiosity is lost. As with life, with storytelling it is the journey that is meaningful, not the destination.** Try telling a punch line without the joke and see how many people are laughing.

14. The Dangers of Being a Scene Fetishist

All too often, when writing a story (or editing footage), a storyteller will invest too much of himself into a single scene or plot point. She will fall in love with a moment and lose sight of the whole. The advice often offered here

175

is sound: **If you find yourself writing and rewriting and the scene works but the story does not, remove that scene.** Put your story back together without what you loved most, and, very often, et voila, the story is back on track again.

Do not be a scene fetishist. No tale rests on one moment. Following the rigor of the craft can be heartbreaking, but you need to buck up, chump. Cut out the scene you adore, step back, and see how the story flows without it. I will not be the first to state that sometimes, falling in love can just flat-out stink.

It actually can be a danger if a scene seems so well conceived that it wants to stand out on its own. If so, the scene probably belongs in another story where it will work as a part of a whole. The scenes in the movie you are presently crafting need to be interdependent, not independent, and each scene, each moment, must make progress towards the climactic moment.

You are the writer. You decide who, what, when, and how. But you are chained to the internal logic of your tale. Each moment in the tale needs justification for inclusion, and not just in terms of whether it is an entertaining moment. Having the female love interest step out of her heels and drop her clothes usually will satisfy the great god Entertainment. Your main consideration, however, must be about how the scene impacts the entire story. Why? Because that is also how your audience will judge your story once the sexy moment has passed. **No scene can make up for a lack of story.**

15. Foreplay And The Cuddling After

Alfred Hitchcock fits the definition of a commercial filmmaker as much as any director in history, but he understood that a carving knife biting into human flesh is not the critical moment.

The audience might think that this is why they bought their tickets, but the professional knows it is not. Hitchcock relishes the foreplay and after-play, but not so much the act itself. The audience rarely gets to see the really "tasty bits" in a Hitchcock film. Hitch tends to cut away, as he did in Frenzy, tracking with the killer right to the door of the victim's apartment –and then tracking right back down the stairs and out into the street where children play, while inside another victim is being strangled. Or he cuts to a bird singing gloriously on a branch, as the alabaster neck of a delicate young lady is being squeezed. Hitch still manages to scare the living daylights out of an audience. It is hard to argue that any other film director could scare an audience more deliciously. You cannot argue with success and yet, it was intrinsic to Hitchcock's storytelling methodology to NOT actually depict those nasty, naughty, "tasty bits."

Note: Scaring the hell out of ourselves is also probably a human need, which is why it is so damn entertaining.

What happens before and after the violence, the sex, or any single plot point, is where a story lives or dies. This is the internal logic of storytelling that Hitchcock understood so well. Portraying the violence or the sex directly can actually stop a story in its tracks. It need not, of course, but there is always that clear and present danger.

If you do not need to include something, anything, in your tale –do not. You are not skydiving. Why risk sudden story-death? This principle stands for any story element, including any scene, or element within a scene. This is not about Puritanism. I am not saying do not explicitly portray a murder or sex. **I am suggesting to add only what needs to be there, and nothing more. Nothing. There is no neutral. Whatever you add will either help or harm your tale.**

It is always about what makes a story better. Again, this suggests that a scene should not stand alone. A scene does, however, need a set-up and a pay-off. You cannot eliminate the set-up or the pay-off (also known as the consequences). So as you write, do the job, do it imaginatively, and do it efficiently. Then move on. Throughout, keep the audience hungry to find out what happens. Keep them a little hungry until the end.

Learn from Hitchcock. For him the sexual event, or violent event, was only an animal act. He was a good Catholic lad but he is not moralizing. In any story, this is but a plot point. In the great scheme of things, this animal act is unimportant, even if for the animal, it is very important. For a lioness, killing an impala is meaningful and just because she needs to feed herself and her family. But lions ask no Big Questions and lions tell no tales. Storytelling is a human thing.

Humans tell tales and require tales. For lions, once their physical appetites and instinctive needs are satisfied, they are satisfied. Lions have little interest in the great scheme of things. For humans, this subject is absolutely compelling. Ask Adam and Eve. Humans require more than bread alone.

16. Writing To Entertain

It is the writer's job to mine life's experiences for value and meaning. That is a calling. When that calling is approached in an audience-centric way, what results can be entertainment.

Entertainment: a term that is widely misunderstood and abused. Most often, entertainment is spun as what "normal people" are after in a book, play, or a movie. That is counter posed to movies with messages, arguments, philosophy, psychology, ethics, insight, metaphysics, or politics, as if these were subjects that only weirdos, wannabe eggheads, and authentic eggheads could care about. Then there are movies that ordinary folks supposedly are interested in –by which is implied, those who work for a living, drink beer, take out the garbage, change diapers, or take the kids to soccer.

Much advice to aspiring scriptwriters is predicated upon this false dichotomy. You have heard it before. There are the writers and filmmakers who live here in the real world where art hits the hard rocky shore of business. They get paid. Then there are the rest, with sugar plum fairies dancing before their eyes. They need a day job. The common advice: The business of making a movie should be your primary concern, and only occasionally should you indulge the luxury of flirting with art. Why even occasionally? Because winning an Oscar is very good for business.

Bottom line: Do you want a seat on the bus, or in a Maserati?

In the trades and screenwriter magazines, the above tends to be ritualistically repeated so many times that

179

most people accept it as gospel. The article of faith is that: Only a small elite are obsessed with such airy-fairy stuff as "meaning." Terms like "real people" and "soccer moms" are trotted out to describe the masses who, supposedly, go to movies not to gain insight, or explore where meaning dwells in their lives, but to escape from their lives and retreat, as children do, into fantasy.

It is as if there is a class of flag-waving dunderheads who buy life off the Wal-Mart rack and demand to just be entertained. These dunderheads, or so goes the rant, do not want or need to find out anything about themselves. They like their "unexamined lives" just fine, thank you very much, and do not give a rat's fart for what the spoiled brat elites think are the finer things in life. Call these supposed dunderheads "ordinary folk." The so-called "spoiled brat elites" might breathe rarified cultural air, but most of us do not live their privileged lives. We do not get the luxury of introspection. Do we?

The truth is that this nonsense, condescension and class bias is rarely coming from those supposedly artsy-fartsy types who doggedly pursue the grail of meaning. On the contrary, it comes more often from hacks who work in what is called the "entertainment industry." Basically, this is their spin. They are the supposed authorities, not because they have facts to defend their opinions, but due to the dubious, "if-you're-so-smart-why-aren't-you-rich" logic.

I do not share this negative assessment of so-called "ordinary people." I do not accept a dichotomy that juxtaposes form against content –"form" being what supposedly entertains people (such as graphic portrayals of sex or explosions) and "content" being what allows for insight into life. Both are necessary. In fact, both are always what you get with a "good tale, well told."

I especially reject the notion that counter poses meaning to fun. This is the idea that most people want fun, and only a few weirdos want meaning. Utter nonsense. This is not what is going on. **Meaning and fun are not just compatible, they are both absolutely necessary to storytelling. They support each other. They are partners in a dancing dialectic.**

Without the fun factor, no one is interested. Without the meaning factor, no one is satisfied. Meaning and fun are two sides of the same coin. It should go without mentioning, but it does not, that what is fun for five year olds is usually is boring to ten year olds and is completely without interest to sixty year olds. Know who your audience is, and deliver meaning and fun. A film that is all eye-candy and style (all form) is a poor film. A film that tries to be deeply meaningful but is boring to watch (all content) is a poor film.

The notion that all "ordinary folks" want is to be put on a wild amusement ride is, at best, mistaken, and, at worst, a license to make bad movies. People believe, on average, what they have been socialized to believe. In this case it is that all they want from movies is escape. But the evidence does not support this notion. The evidence is that most of the biggest box office hits, the Oscar winners, deliver both. They are captivating, and thus entertaining; and they deliver insight. The particular genre of the book or the film is irrelevant. No matter the genre, you have to deliver both fun and insight. The same goes for writing a comedy or tragedy. The great classic Hollywood films like Gone with the Wind, Grand Hotel, Casablanca, It Happened One Night, Best Days of Our Lives,

181

The Great Escape, The Godfather, and so many others, all shed light on the big issues of life. All captivate their audiences. All are great fun to watch.

I list those examples because they are all marvels, and their stories are all over the map in terms of style and genre. They were all moneymakers. I limit myself to classic Hollywood films only out of expediency. Thousands of wonderful films and novels have been written since the studio era. **The much-wooed mainstream audience wants a chance to escape all right, but to an alternative universe where they can be viscerally tested and confront life's dragons from a comfortable, seated position.**

That, for them, is fun. Therefore, we can boldly go where few have ever gone before, and state forthrightly that the same goes for one and all. If a "serious" film does not entertain its intended audience, it is a failure. We have come full circle.

Never underestimate your audience. Write about what matters to them. Do not condescend. If you are not empathetic with the aspirations, disappointments, anxieties, or sensibilities of your target demographic, find an audience you can write for.

I am no more against escapist storytelling than I am against ice cream. Give your audience a thrilling, rollicking good time. Build them a star-gate. Put them on the bridge of a submarine. Allow them to make torrid love on a tropical beach with the most beautiful person in the world. Propel them at warp speed to other solar systems. Help them escape drudgery, repetition, and lethargy; but do not provide a means to escape the truth. **The prime directive is not to build an escape hatch, but to build a bridge and thereby lend wings to the**

imagination and send your audience on a journey to the land of What Matters. We look to nonfiction to get at facts. We employ fiction to get at truth.

What really matters to all of us is to lead fulfilling lives in our present reality. Your duty as a storyteller is to challenge and shatter delusions about reality, but to do so, as much as you are able to, without prejudice. You cannot write good fiction if you write propaganda. You also cannot write objective truth; it is just not available to us mere mortals. What does that leave you? With the twin virtues, honesty and courage.

The truth is elusive, but you can be honest, although that takes courage. Write from honesty. Be as honest and as clear as you are able, and shed light on the truth that you cannot articulate. Do not do the opposite. Do not evoke the dark art. Never be an enabler of the retreat into infantilism and denial –even if that is a common human impulse. Remember what is incumbent on a true magus. And that also includes a duty to entertain.

In Genesis, when Adam and Eve took a bite from the fruit of the Tree of Knowledge, they created the human condition. Notice, please, this was not the Tree of Delusion. They did not take a bite of that apple. It was knowledge that they tasted. Not a lot but, evidently, enough to get them hoofed out of the state of innocence, where fulfillment is automatic and free.

I would contend that the pursuit of the truth is the prize, not the punishment, of sentience. Films such as Palm Beach Story, Breakfast at Tiffany's, High Noon, The Apartment, Rosemary's Baby, The Godfather, Batman: The Dark Knight –all popular hits, all moneymakers– were also effective at getting at universal truths about our lives. Some of that truth was bitter, some of it sweet. It makes little difference: Our species seem to hunger for this fruit the way other critters such as dogs, snakes, tuna fish, or spiders seemingly do not. Of all kinds of knowledge, self-knowledge is probably the end-goal. We may hop aboard the Starship Enterprise with the stated goal of traveling to distant galaxies, but the real quest is to find ourselves. That is what matters to us. We are not omniscient gods; and maybe because we are not gods, we make art, we tell stories. We tell stories to get at truths that we cannot seem to get at any other way. Considering that "truth," the word, "entertainment," takes on a different meaning.

If you want my definition of writing to entertain, here it is: Writing in an entertaining way merely means to write in such a way that the audience has been manipulated, through craft, to buy into a story.

17. You Can Run Out Of Plots But Never Stories

Storytelling is fundamental for our species. You might say it is in our DNA. Without stories and storytelling, everything that happens in the human journey is in danger of just becoming passing scenery on our way to our own inevitable Act III.

The good news is that we will not run out of stories, as long as storytellers possess insight and creativity. We can, however, run out of basic plots. Depending on what expert you are referring to, the number of basic plots has been said to range from two to about 100. This should not be taken too seriously. A lot of the difference is dependent on what is considered a basic plot. **What seems irrefutable is that there are not that many basic plots, and that you can build any plot out of various combinations of off-the-shelf ingredients such as violence, sex, and death.** Of course, it is just as true that all that exists is but positive or negative charges on electrons. The permutations in both cases are just about infinite. **But just remember, a plot is not a story.**

The boy-meets-girl category of plots have been worked and reworked thousands of times. The number of variations is almost endless. Here is one: Girl meets boy, Girl likes Boy, Boy really likes Girl, Girl and Boy enter a romantic and sexual relationship. Girl eventually becomes dissatisfied with Boy. Girl attempts to mold Boy into something more pleasing to Girl. Girl realizes (usually not soon enough) that Boy is not made out of clay. Boy is cast in concrete and so Boy concludes that he needs a Girl who loves him for just being him.

Here is another one: It is similar to the previous example, but this time it's Girl who concludes that changing Boy is a Sisyphean task –an impossible and unrewarding enterprise. She discovers there is no depth to Boy, despite the fact that he is pretty. So Girl gives Boy the bum's rush out the door. Time to eat ice cream out of the carton, and then move on.

More variations: Boy and Girl have what is, for the most part, a solid relationship. But Girl's parents connive to undermine their relationship. Boy's parents? Why not? So, do Boy and Girl have the intestinal fortitude to face down Big Bad Dragon Mother and Silver-haired, Sociopath, Martini-swilling Dad? What if the stakes are that Boy will never see his family again? They are very rich and they will cut Boy off. Boy intends well, but he is spoiled. Boy, is he spoiled! But he does not know it, and this plot now seems to be heading towards tragedy. In the comic version, Boy does know he is spoiled, admits it, and loves it. (Perfect example: the classic romantic comedy, Arthur.) In any event, does Boy have any marketable skills? Will he make it through massage therapy school? Will he fall in love with the gorgeous young rich girl he gives a massage to, someone who would be absolutely acceptable to his parents, but someone who is not Girl? Shall we test his mettle?

Or maybe Girl discovers that it is Boy's Bad-Boy Brother whom she cannot resist. She thought she was in love with Boy, but now she falls into the real deal. Or not. Or she just thinks she falls in love. Maybe it is just great sex that is better than with Boy. In any case, poor Goody-Two-Shoes brother named Boy is out of luck.

Then again, we could make Girl the Churchy Goody-Two-Shoes.

Or maybe not. Maybe Girl is a reformed drug addict. Has she kept that from Boy? How reformed is she really? Is Girl about to relapse? Or will Boy save her from herself? Shall we test the mettle of both of them? We can.

Or, Boy could be on his way to becoming a priest, and, what do you know, Girl announces she's pregnant. (Ah, the perils of the "rhythm method.")

What if Boy is a prodigy, seemingly destined to become a world famous concert violinist? We can contrive it so that staying with Girl means sacrificing his dream. Again, we can throw in Baby. Like biblical Delilah, maybe her job is to take away his power and his future. No reason that Girl cannot be an antagonist.

Or, returning to the "bun in the oven" plot-device, and employing a different twist: Girl is against abortion and Boy is for it. He is for it, but in this version, he is about to become a Catholic priest.

Or, or, or...

Does not matter. We have seen or read it all before. But we have exhausted nothing. **If you have the insight, creativity, and the right chops, there is no reason you cannot write another girl-meets-boy story.** The magic will renew. The audience is reborn a virgin every time they take a seat in the theater. Do your job right, and it will always seem to them to be the first time.

Plot is not where you have to worry about being original. It is the interplay between plot and story that is the playground for good writers. Every plot is a cow milked for centuries, and yet the cow remains productive. She is a magic cow –if you know how to milk her, that is. If you do not, she will send you flying into the manure pile with a swift kick.

Any failure to make a plot into a new story is yours alone. Until the human race definitively figures out what they are, who they are, and what they are supposed to be doing while they are here, writers need not worry. We are nowhere near exhausting all the good story ideas.

To make an old plot into a new story, you need to do more than rearrange plot elements. (Note, please, I refrain from using the phrase, "invent plot elements," because it is unlikely that you can come up with any that are not ancient.) Just as important is for a writer to work out how the protagonist responds to the challenges you have provided for them in Act II. You provided these challenges through every writer's secret agent, the villain or antagonist. I am referring here to psychology, credible psychology. This means developing a psychological profile for your main characters, and especially for the hero. What are her weaknesses and what are her strengths? Most critically, what does she need to learn to slay her dragon? Your protagonist(s) and your antagonist(s) should come across as three dimensional, flesh and blood human beings. Even the most unusual and heroic of heroes, or the nastiest of villains, should feel human to the audience.

The magic is right there, in the psychology, not the plot. Plots are easy and cheap, as I tried to demonstrate earlier in this chapter. Flesh and blood characters that an audience identifies with are dear –meaning, in terms of the insight and effort required from you to make them, expensive. **Those who simply push two-dimensional, paper-doll character clichés through a snake-and-ladders plot of memes do not rise above mediocrity.**

No matter how many ways you blow things up, or the number of explicitly portrayed sexual positions, there will come a point where your story fails. Why? Because you ignored character development.

Storytelling is about humans searching for real meaning and true value in the time between their first breath and their last. Ever since humans became self-aware and sentient; ever since Eve and Adam ostensibly sucked the blood-red juices from the pomegranate that God, or ostensibly that God, dangled before them; ever since then, that has been the job of storytelling. Certain topics are almost universally of interest to us hapless, hairless apes with big brains. They all come down to love of one kind or another –romantic love being just one variation. But if ground zero is the mystery of love, next to ground zero is this other mystery: Given that at some time in the future, there will be no you, why care about anything that happens after the moment of your nonexistence? Since so much of life seems to be unfulfilling, if not downright disappointing, why, for example, make children? Why bother with anything difficult, or at least anything difficult that does not make money? And once you have money, why not just have fun, or why not just achieve a state of blotto? Someone please pass me the whiskey bottle.

At times, most people, and that includes storytellers, tend to speculate darkly about how life is a meaningless farce. For some writers, everything is hollow; all that is, is surface; and so on. Everything they write is tongue-in-cheek, and everything they write is "within quotes." The best they can be is clever, and for some, every story that comes out of them is farce. For others, they either drink themselves to death, or commit an alternative kind of suicide, or they surface and start writing.

You can, of course, choose to write farce. Nothing wrong with a good farce. Farce is just another genre. Some write well within that genre, but they use the genre to get at the Big Issues. That is what is meant by writing fiction well, period. It is also true that some writers –why lie, a great many writers– live in a very dark abode. But good writers drag themselves out of their caves. They have to. There is something arrogant, not so much about speculating darkly, but about arriving at a definitive cynical conclusion. It is just too easy. It stinks of hubris. It implies throwing in the towel, backing away from the job. It is the difference between cynicism and skepticism. Cynics know. Skeptics question. Cynics typically relish any opportunity to dampen the spirits of the obstinate seekers of light. But the obstinate seeker has an answer as she slogs past the cynic up the hill again. Is there any other choice? But really, this is a rhetorical quest, and she is asking this of herself. All good writers are skeptics.

It will turn out that the slain serpent had buried her eggs, and soon they hatch, and we are slogging back up that mountain again to slay the serpent one more time. The effort, however, is worth it. The journey is always meaningful, and if you, the storyteller, can combine the obstinate effort with the right skills (and if you have earned your dollop of insight) there will be an audience for your work. The audience, too, has what the psychologist William James (brother to Henry, the famous storyteller) termed "the obstinate desire to think clearly" –even if they are not fully aware of that desire just yet.

This is why finding meaning in the boy-girl tango is of abiding interest to almost everybody. It is hypnotic. **Finding meaning matters to all of us, even if that meaning seems to deepen, undulate, shift, and dance over time. As we clever apes with big brains gather ever more data about ourselves and the universe, nothing changes about the quest for meaning.** Nothing is quelled. Every question science answers seems to hatch a dozen sprightly new ones. In ancient lore, the serpent represents, among other things, wisdom. Perhaps it is time to re-evaluate the snake God places in the garden.

Science is perpetually imperfect, a work in progress, a great and noble calling; but only art can be perfect –even if flawed, perfect. In this sense, Van Gogh's "Starry Night" is perfect, even if the artist was a deeply flawed, despondent man.

Science is after fundamental principles of nature, which should not be confused with finding meaning. E=MC2 is perplexing and fascinating, even if it may not even be the ultimate truth. Did you know, however, that Einstein could not get out of his head a girl who he barely glimpsed the night before he came up with that equation? This happened in a bar. He did not talk to her, but her dress brushed him, as he was hunched over on a bar deep in his head ruminating over science. The girl turned around, her blue eyes met his brown eyes ... and then she left the bar, but she never left his mind. She was a pretty girl, but not more so than many other young ladies. Why her? As Albert lay dying in a hospital bed, going in and out of consciousness, and when he could still pick up his writing pad to scribble equations with the stub of a pencil in a final attempt to prove the General Theory of Relativity, his mind instead kept flashing to her. She was getting in the way. She was the last thing he saw. His last thought? Why her? If not for her, maybe he could have figured it out.

Of course, this is fiction. I am making this up. I am only telling a story. In fact, I am beginning one. Do you want to know "why her"? I have answers.

Meaning is the province of the arts, and meaning is chimeric. Meaning seems to elude logic, yet cannot contradict it. Meaning is not anti-logical, but logic cannot fetch meaning. It does seem as if something at bottom remains a constant, the way E=MC2 is supposedly also a codification of a constant. But what does that mean?

Consider the old boy-girl tango a dance towards meaning. Spice it up. Toss in a pinch of the absurd as two people dance the one-beast-with-two-backs tango, and audience interest will likely become compulsive. **You got them. You have hooked them by their hormones and their instincts. Now what? If this dance is to rise from**

191

an event to storytelling material, this can only go one place, to the link between pleasure and happiness, and the difference; to the link between animal and spiritual, and the difference. The difference is the romance. Theme, theme, and more theme!

Adam and Eve, having eaten of the Tree of Knowledge, apple juice dripping off their chins, discover that they are in quite the pickle jar, all righty. Mind has just been born as somehow separate from brain, spirit has just been born as somehow separate from body, and who we really are is seemingly separated from what we appear to be: hairless apes.

For some cultures, being a hairless ape is something shameful; for others, not so much. In fact, they might celebrate the naked hairless human body, as the Greeks did, before the rise of Christianity. It should not come as an astonishing insight that this dilemma, this dichotomy, has been a subject of storytelling for, as near as we can tell, all of human existence. Call it the romance genre, if you like. It is but one storytelling genre, and they all have been with us for a very long time.

There is an ancient Persian tale we know as the One Thousand and One Nights. One of those stories is about a young street thief named Aladdin who, by being clever, gains entrance to the cave of a fellow called Ali Baba. The cave is full of heaps of precious gems, gold, and all that glitters. But the one item that is of true value is a common enough looking oil lamp that is dull and dented.

If it is true that "all that glitters is not gold," it is just as true that what really matters rarely glitters at all. You must possess certain inner qualities to perceive that truth. Rarely do the virtues such as courage, honesty, selflessness, generosity, fairness, and most important of all, kindness, shine out at you. The journey to virtue describes the story-arch of a petty thief and street urchin named Aladdin. When the protagonist, Aladdin, transforms himself, it is not the genie's doing, it is Aladdin's doing. Once he finally proves that he is truly virtuous he gains the hand of the princess and becomes king of the land. They live happily ever after, as does the kingdom.

Aladdin is like that dull dented lamp. That metaphor is not accidental. The moral of this story might be stated as: There is a genie inside all of us, but it is up to us to let it out. This story might come across as an exotic fairytale meant to entertain children, but it is also deep, metaphysical, transformational stuff.

Some tales are less superficial than others. Some are boring. Some are riveting. Nevertheless, sneaking into Ali Baba's Magic Cave and finding that hidden item of esoteric value is what motivates all good writers, even those who do not know it. But it is better to know it. **You can never exhaust that cave. It is brimming with treasures, plot-devices, violence, sex, adventure, intrigue; but there is probably only one item of true and lasting value in it – and it is never the one that shines.**

18. Ali Baba's Magic Cave And What Does Not Shine In It

On Hollywood's Poor Little Rich Girl/Rich Little Poor Girl Stories

In Hollywood, Poor Little Rich Girl, or Boy, stories abound. (Again, I refer you to Arthur.) These films tend

193

to be about a girl (or a boy) being surrounded by life's material advantages (the shiny stuff) and yet all that luxury, indulgence, pleasure, and pampering has no lasting value for the Poor Little Rich Girl. She is poor of spirit, alas. Something more valuable than all she has is missing. What is it? Where is it?

Again, this is really testing the theme concerning the difference between pleasure and happiness.

On the other side of the coin, Rich Little Poor Girl stories are almost as plentiful. (Coal Miner's Daughter, Hugo). These tales tend to be predicated on the rather droll notion that, just because she (or he) comes into the world with few material advantages, and earning a living is not easy, happiness and lasting value nevertheless lie right before her eyes, if she would only open them. We now only need to invent the plot, the Act II, where she opens them, or not.

Rich Little Poor Girl tales are about how Poor Girl comes to the realization that she is actually rich. Hollywood surrounds Rich Little Poor Girl with a loving if quirky character-rich family and neighborhood, while by comparison, the mansion in which Poor Little Rich Girl lives is empty and desolate.

This stuff is Hollywood boilerplate, and has been milked for years by producers in search of the glittery stuff. Few of these Hollywood cigar chomping producers, however, have gone for Poor Little Poor Girl stories. They leave these slice-of-life tales to independent, or foreign filmmakers. They tend to consider it dull, dismal fare. Too bleak for American audiences.

Dismal, maybe, but there is nothing boring about films such as Francoise Truffaut's French New Wave tragedy, The 400 Blows (Les Quatre Cents Coups.) Just be aware that you might be swimming against the current when shopping a Poor Little Poor Girl script around Tinsel Town. The nickname exists for a reason and yet, as I suggested at the beginning of this book, some of the greatest American classic movies are variations of the Poor Little Poor Girl plot. Director William Wyler's stark The Best Years Of Our Lives stole the 1946 Oscar for Best Picture from what might be Frank Capra's finest film. It's A Wonderful Life is a stellar example of the Rich Little Poor Boy subgenre. Talk about earning your Hollywood Ending.

19. Happiness

Really, it all boils down to this one Big Question: Where dwells human happiness? This is the mother of all storytelling dragons, and really she is the singular dragon that all writer-Jacks are employed to confront and slay. Rich or poor, old or young, healthy in the prime of life or gravely ill near the end, all humans search for happiness, and storytelling exists for that reason.

When you flee from the truth, the reason might be symptomatic of a neurotic condition, and the most common truth people fear probably is something they are repressing about themselves. The problem is that what we fear often is manifested, but the monster is usually in the mirror. If we do not know that we are gazing in the mirror, the result can be what the acid generation called a "bad trip."

This kind of confrontation is what psychologist Carl Jung claimed is between you and your own shadow. Most of us are, in this sense, afraid of our own shadows. Jung, however, contended that in the right circumstances, such a confrontation can set you on the road to happiness. But fear is fear. Fear is part of the human condition. Without fear, there cannot be heroism. Many neurotics, possibly most of us, would rather remain huddled in a cave, watching the kind of reality television that is as far from reality as can be contrived. The audience for what is, in the worst sense, "escapist entertainment" is so huge that it is difficult not to think of this neurotic tendency to retreat from reality as normal.

Catharsis is the process of releasing, and thereby providing relief from, strong or repressed emotions.

Fortunately, catharsis can be provided through a surrogate and a guided tour though storyland. The surrogate is the story's protagonist. In that sense alone, storytelling is a gift to humanity, from humanity. There is no need to go to war to discover what war is all about.

I have heard it said that the difference between a cat and a human child is that, when a curious child touches a hot stove, she never touches a hot stove again, while once a cat jumps on a hot stove, it never jumps on any stove again, hot or cold. A story provides a means of touching a hot stove without getting burnt. A story can allow you to confront your shadow vicariously and still gain a cathartic moment. Have you ever cried at the end of a movie?

Speaking of shadows, the bittersweet comic film Groundhog Day is an excellent example of a sugar-coated story that takes its protagonist, as our surrogate, on a journey to confront, basically, himself.

Happiness can be a serious business. When you write a script about a Poor Little Poor Girl that accurately portrays the ugliness, inequity, and unfairness that stands between Poor Little Poor Girl and happiness, mainstream Hollywood tends not to be interested, possibly because producers falsely assume that your story would leave the audience depressed and that artsy films are bad box office. They are not entirely wrong, but they are mostly wrong. The Last Picture Show, a 1971 film described as bleak and dismal, was directed by then Hollywood outsider, Peter Bogdanovich. It cost a modest $1.3 million. It received eight Oscar nominations, including Best Picture, and grossed $29 million. That was a fortune in 1971.

Mainstream Hollywood tends to underestimate the box office potential of catharsis, especially when experienced from a comfortable seat. Every once and so often, Hollywood wakes up to rediscover that people will pay the same price for a ticket to laugh or to cry. Robert Benson's 1979 film, Kramer Vs. Kramer, is a nuanced slice-of-life about a divorce. It is, in my opinion, one of the best films ever made, and not just in Hollywood. It is a tear-jerker lacking that supposedly redeeming Hollywood ending. In 1980 it swept the Oscars. It cost $8 million and grossed $173 million.

There are a few Hollywood producers who occasionally will take on such a project on the basis of it being a very strong script, and not only because they are willing to lose money in the cause of seeking that elusive Oscar winner. These things do happen, but keep in mind that every scriptwriter with a similar bee under their bonnet will be vying for the attention of these rare producers.

A tragic ending, when real-life obstacles to happiness are enormous, might be the statistical norm, but not according to Hollywood. Think about it: If abject circumstances were good for you, then being born with AIDS in a rural village in Nigeria would be your special gift. Scripts that tell it like it is tend to be ignored by Hollywood for many reasons, some of them fairly sound. They are risky business. Manchester on the Sea, which won two Oscars, was risky business. The movers and shakers in Hollywood are subject to the same fear-driven neuroses as everyone else. Few of us are truly brave, like cowboy heroes. Sure, we save the day, no matter what negative consequences for ourselves –but only in our heads.

As the popular author of self-help books Eckhart Tolle put it, "The human condition can be described as being lost in your thoughts." Any good story has to break through that mental fog. If all that is accomplished on your hero's journeys is thicker fog; well, you have to understand why producers would reject your script. These kinds of profoundly sad stories must deliver catharsis. There are basic rules of the road for catharsis, even if the outcome of the tale is tragic. There needs to be a realistic plot. The obstacles to happiness must be real. The protagonist needs to be relatable, meaning likable, despite any flaws. Your protagonists do need flaws. This is not just to be relatable, but also to avoid melodrama, which is a looming threat when crafting this kind of tale. The audience responds positively to the flawed hero because he is a victim of insurmountable, vicious circumstances. That said, "bad things happen to good people" is not news, and neither is "good people are not perfect people." That is why, after the climax of the tale, there might not be a dry face in the audience. The message received is: Try your best. Nobody can do more. Thank your lucky stars; your life can be a lot worse. The result is a release of guilt and empathy. You made them cry? Job well done.

Hollywood movies such as Taxi Driver, Chinatown, Brazil, and There Will Be Blood all strike a tone that can be described as nothing short of bleak. Arguably, most of the great movies are colored some shade of bleak. What is considered by many critics as the greatest of all Westerns, High Noon, is extremely stark and bleak in its social criticism. The mainstream audience, it seems, has nothing against a movie without that "feel-good" flavor. Feel bad stories have their place. That kind of storytelling, however, requires enormous skill and insight to achieve broad acclaim. Many such tragedies are only successful, if they are successful, in the art houses, or with what Hollywood calls "niche audiences." This is not at all a terrible outcome for a film –just do not expect to buy yourself a Maserati.

Nevertheless, the myth that the mainstream audience goes to movies for happy endings persists, as does Hollywood executives' prejudice against "downers." There are many reasons for this, but undoubtedly one of them is a disinclination of rich and successful people to acknowledge that fortune and happenstance played a significant role in their success. If they only had the character mettle to accept what is so self-evident, it might help to deflate the ego problem that also persists in Hollywood. But first, they would need to climb out of their heads.

I am compelled to admit that any insight in the above passage is unoriginal. That great collection of stories, the Bible, equates a rich person's chance of going to heaven with a camel's chance of passing through the eye of a needle. If we equate the concept of heaven with enduring happiness, this warning from the Bible is about how your blessings can become your curses.

As the saying goes, "I thought I had it bad since I had no shoes. Then I met a man with no feet." "Hubris" is the name of the sin when you think what you got, you deserve. You deserve what you deserve. Now, how to test for that? Well, this too is storytelling.

Aladdin, in the Disney movie of the same name, had to rub a dented, dull lamp before a genie poofed out of it. The genie granted him three tests, disguised as wishes. The tests were about choosing inner wealth –filed under the categories "love" and "wisdom," collectively "virtue"– over what the great wide world tends to believe is wealth: the glittery stuff.

Had Al, a young man at the bottom of the pecking order, and a petty thief by trade, disobeyed the instructions to take only the dented lamp from the cave and, instead, stuffed his pockets with glittery stuff, then even if his financial problems had been solved, he would not have won the princess. He would not have become a sultan. He would have fallen short in the "virtue" department. He would have proven himself to be of base mettle –and thus, not truly noble.

These tests were not easy to pass for young Al, a child of poverty living in the streets of a rich caliphate where bling was being flashed at him constantly, even when he had nothing to eat. That glittery stuff was tantalizing. All he had to do was develop the skills to snatch it.

So was Al, at core, a hero? Was he, despite his circumstances set out in Act I, a person of the true aristocracy? That kind of person remains virtuous, despite the circumstances. But this is a tale about how to become a hero. Aladdin was not that person at the beginning of the tale, but in Act II, he chooses to slay his personal dragon, and he succeeds. He wins the princess. He wins love and, please note, abiding happiness. "And no sultan ruled as wisely, fairly, and honestly as Sultan Aladdin. And no sultan was more generous to his people." Aladdin, the Disney version.

20. Joe Six Pack And His War Movies

On the far shore, across the emotional sea from the love stories, lie the war stories. They are opposites, or so it seems. In battle, what is important to soldiers, and to armchair warriors, is that the wheat of what counts remains, and the chaff of what is unimportant and gets in the way, is blown to smithereens. **Boom! The battle, or series of battles, provides the meat of almost every Act II in a war story. The action, however, is only the action. Either it is gratuitous, or it gets at the theme.**

Every good war story is also a relationship story. Will the protagonist face down death to watch his buddy's back? Will they be there for each other? War is where you get down to it. Do you have the skills, the character, the guts, and the heart to do what needs to be done when the time comes? Or will you freeze up, or run away? **What needs to be addressed is why you have the right stuff, not just how.**

"How" is a plot question. "Why" is a theme question. Can you, the storyteller, shed light on the "why"?

War is the situation in Act I. War serves to strip away all pretense and conceit in the face of possible, perhaps imminent, death in Act II. Battle is a mechanism that delivers an in-your-face test of the blood and grit of character. The driving force for all good war stories is who is truly virtuous, and who does not have it. The exterior can be impressive, while the interior can be hollow. Who's got it? What is the difference between bravado and bravery? Let's find out.

By the climax of Act II, some have risen up and others have fallen, and in a good war story, like any tale well told, not necessarily the most deserving survive – in fact sometimes, it's the opposite. This is also true of love stories. **Not every protagonist, or antagonist, necessarily ends up where the audience wants them to end up in Act III. But in the telling of the story, the virtuous are always revealed, while those lacking virtue are also**

revealed. In this sense, the theater of love is not that different from the theater of war.

Allow me to be audacious and politically incorrect enough to suggest that Joe Six Pack tends to go to a romantic movie only because a significant female wants to, and probably as foreplay. I am not suggesting this as criticism. Just who goes to what films and why has been studied to death. For Hollywood, this is a money question. Although this is generalizing, I do not believe that it is an unfair assessment –but neither is the statement that this does not work the other way around. Few women allow themselves to be dragged to a war movie, especially if it is bloody and violent.

That war movies tend to skew towards males, while romance movies skew towards females, is a tawdry observation. It is not so tawdry to note that war stories are as centered around relationships as romance stories. The plot in the war genre, despite the bing-bang-boom of the action and profuse amounts of bloodshed, is a journey towards heroism, punctuated by tension-building scenes of what might be described as intimate banter. Again, this is not substantially different from how the plot works in a successful romance.

Here is a unifying principle: All plots must serve to test the character mettle of protagonists, whether lovers or soldiers.

I doubt it is news to anyone that the war genre portrays the psychology of males much the way romance genre does the same for females, and probably no less or no more accurately. There are attitudinal differences between the genders, but this is not the place to debate how many are because of nature and how many are the result of nurture. **Suffice it to say that, as a professional**

writer, you need to connect to the psychology of readers and viewers. If they trend male, then this observation is going to be especially salient for you: men tend to open up to each other in war, as they also do in the arena of mock war, sports. Say what you want, but the romance genre does not tend to draw in males as much. Perhaps this is because these kinds of stories are less cathartic for most men. The need for cathartic release, however, transcends gender.

Perhaps it is controversial for me to say this, and I will concede that gender roles seem to be evolving; nonetheless, in my experience, on humdrum home fronts such as a marital spat, many men withdraw, clam-like, into an emotional shell. Either that or they lash out in one way or another. Maybe it is innate, or maybe it is just how our society operates, but, generally speaking, women are given license to express their emotions. Men, not so much. The only negative emotion many men allow themselves to express is anger. Anger is certainly not the entirety of what is going on within men, but to put it bluntly, men are often emotionally stunted. If this makes some men brutes, it might free others from the entanglement of the emotional empathetic web, so that they can do what men historically have had to do –which is some form of head chopping, whether in war, sports, or in the office.

If you have a war story percolating, you will need to intercept male psychology as it is. Storytellers reach people where they are. This does not mean that the people you want to connect with know where they are. Even if the target audience for war movies tends to insist that they go to movies "just to be entertained," you need to disregard that little word, "just." No one, men, women or children, goes to movies "just to be entertained." They are not liars, but the term is so trite as to be rendered almost worthless. We go to movies, or read books, just as much to be edified as thrilled. **If you are trying to be a "real man", this might not be so easy to admit. What is it, do you think, that these "real men" fear? That is definitely worth addressing in your fiction.**

The quote "War Is hell" is attributed to the Civil War general, William Tecumseh Sherman. He was not only a man who knew hell, he was a man who brought hell. Most of the people who first go to this hell as boys, full of puff and glory, either earn their stripes to become "real men" on the field of battle, or they do not. Some of the best war movies depict that process. You might say that young men go to war as so many marching Little Red Riding Hoods. You might also say that many of the men who go to war movies do so as so many sitting Little Red Riding Hoods. The best of these war stories disaffect them of their naiveté. The worst deepen their illusions and serve as recruitment tools. Some eat the wolf and others are eaten by the wolf.

The protagonist character arcs depicted in expertly made war movies, such as The Grand Illusion, Bridge Over the River Kwai, Lawrence of Arabia, Apocalypse Now, Cross of Iron, The Deer Hunter, Enemy at the Gate, and Saving Private Ryan, reveal the mettle of their protagonists as subtle, multi-layered, and often contradictory. You, as the writer, definitely need the warrior stuff; and in between, you need the normal fare, such as: banter between characters, playful ribbing, camaraderie, friendships, rivalries, longing for home and family, and so on. You need the humanizing stuff, set against the dehumanizing stuff. You need moral conflict just as much as the conflict of battle. You need fear because no one is a hero who is not afraid. You need fears that are overcome, and fears to which the character succumbs. You need be-loved characters doing what is wrong just as much as you need them doing what is right, especially at those decisive moments in battle. Fortunately for writers of war stories, these decisive moments arise in droves. Just understand that decisive moments do not stand alone. You cannot make a war movie, or at least not a good one, out of only decisive moments. **The intimate depiction of male psychology opening up under duress in these stories provides the contrasting background for the violence in the foreground. Remember, your job is to illuminate the truth.**

By comparison, for a successful romance, that lingering mooshy movie kiss, so tedious for many males, is a man-datory prequel to the consummation of the relationship in the physical act of making love for most of the females in the audience. The triumph of "true love" is the result of a journey towards honesty and courage in the face of the cold reality of alienation, loneliness, and pain. The climax needs to be a breakthrough. The lingering kiss, and other mooshy parts of a romance story, speak to a spiritual union, not just a physical union. That consti-tutes the background, enabling us to see that finding love and intimacy is something that has to be earned through the exercise of virtue. True love is not something that just happens to a girl or a boy. Otherwise, there would be no tale to tell. And anyway, it is rarely true in life either.

Why sacrifice for others, or for a cause? Why risk your life? Is not your life all you really have? Anything that is not shedding light on the "why" in the storytelling will just be a sequence of tawdry or superficial events that, at best, might excite the hormones of lust or fear. Nev-ertheless, they will be "full of sound and fury, signifying nothing," as The Bard said.

Hormones drive people to have sex. Hormones drive people to violence. Hormones, however, explain how, not why. They are part of a biological mechanism and serve to demonstrate that people, too, are animals driven by evolution to survive and procreate. This is factual, but it is only a part of the truth about what is going on within us. This is just a scientific observation, and an incomplete one at that. There is no meaning here and so, nothing worthy of a story. Hormones are not a theme, but humans can and do override their hormones, and that makes us at least a little different from every other animal we know of. The human animal can choose to go on a diet, and sometimes even choose to stick with it. Can a dog?

That we can, and often do, choose to override our natural proclivities and that hat this happens unspectacularly, speaks to the fact of our sentience. **This does not just imply. It shouts that providing insight into what makes us human and, out of that, the deep and obsessive interest in character development that follows, is of prime interest to storytellers. This is not to suggest that plot is irrelevant; rather, it means that character development through character testing IS the plot. Plots should not be reduced to a sequence of events.**

An overemphasis on plot, at the expense of character development, will lead, at best, to mediocrity. Yet in my experience, if you ask many writers to explain what their tales are about, they will outline the plot. It takes courage to resist the spin out there, even if you suspect that maybe there is something wrong with the conventional way that stories are being told, and valued. **Most of us go with the flow. Most of us shy away from asking the**

Big Questions. Most of us should not be professional storytellers.

21. Thanatos And Eros – And Doctor Sigmund Freud

Freud was a secular Jew, and educated in the Talmud. The Talmud, an artifact of particularly the European Jewish tradition, consists of about 6200 pages of insight and wisdom, and is no light read. Somewhere within those 6200 pages, the Talmud refers to death as the portal of illumination, and thus final darkness gives birth to endless light. That idea is a dialectic, meaning two seeming opposites comprising one whole.

A similar notion is also rooted in classical Greek thought. This is no coincidence. The medieval scholars who established the European Jewish tradition had been seduced by Classical Greek thinking. That body of knowledge had been lost in Europe after Rome fell, but had been preserved in North Africa. At the zenith of expanding Islamic civilization, those ideas returned to Europe with the Moorish conquest of Spain. The rediscovery of Classical Greek culture and thought in Europe is when, many believe, the light was lit that ended the European Dark Ages and began the Renaissance.

There is a great story here, in fact many; but this is not the place to tell any of them. Suffice it to state, it was no coincidence that Freud first identified the elemental, seductive attraction of death as the corollary to the seductive power of the life force, or Eros. Eros is a Greek goddess and Thanatos, a Greek demi-god. Freud, however, used the German term Todestriebe rather than

Thanatos, which was first coined from the Greek by one of his followers.

Thanatos is the term now used, and the idea is important no less to psychologists than it is to storytellers. What is most important to understand is that these are twin forces that constitute two parts of one whole. For storytellers who want to develop living, breathing characters, these two forces must be at work within them as well. Both psychologists and storytellers are dealing with the human condition; wrestling it to the ground, so to speak.

Freud contends that both Thanatos and Eros toil away within a normal human psyche, but neurosis results when they fight each other, instead of working together as one. According to Freud, neurosis is a form of mental distress that generates depression and unhappiness. Healing mental distress was the locus of the good doctor's work. His famous way of treating his patients was to drag what was at work within the darkness of their unconscious into the light of consciousness. He called that process "psychoanalysis."

Freud's healing process parallels the process of storytelling, an insight that did not escape him; and neither should this insight escape you, the storyteller. Where abides happiness, and how to attain it, is at the core of every good tale. This was as much the case in Classical Greece as it is now. All Greek drama, all their literature, and all their philosophy is about that. All their great stories and plays speak to us still, dissolving the millennia between their era and our own. All their tales have three dimensional protagonists moving through three acts, with both shadow and light at work within them. All these protagonists, in one way or another, strive from Act II to attain happiness, although not always primarily for themselves. Some fail, some succeed, and most end up somewhere in between.

Greek drama gives birth to the Shakespearean play and to the fictional narrative form we call a novel, which emerges around the same time. These two art forms combine to give birth to the screenplay and filmmaking.

Freud's insight into human beings resonates with Plato's definition of human beings: an angel chained to a demon. I mentioned this notion previously. There is a lot of evidence supporting both theories, but this is not what we should be dwelling on in a how-to about storytelling. A how-to should be practical, even this one. But there is a practical matter herein– in fact, a few.

One is that, as a practical matter, war stories cannot only star Thanatos. Shadow and light are inseparable in life, and even more so when it is life and death. There cannot be one without the other. They constitute one phenomenon.

Thanatos is the shadow of Eros. This means that, in order to create the character-arcs for those who are fighting in a war, the attraction of life must be at work within them, along with the attraction of death. Ideally, that will be evident in the writing, the acting, the cinematography, and the directing.

At the climax, cigarette smoldering and machine gun blazing, the soldier-hero saves the day by charging the enemy against insurmountable odds, but he is shot. Oh, no! He staggers but continues, he drops four enemies for every shot his body takes, but he is hit again, and again, until he falls ... And yet he rises up again and charges, as if he has not been hurt at all; "the force" seems to be with him, and hope is renewed in the audience. Except the hero is hit again, and now his left arm dangles lifeless, so he continues shooting with his right arm, until he is shot again and collapses to his knees. He struggles to stand up and he does, except, wham, he is hit right in the middle of his heroic chest, and hope dies in the audience as the reality of war is sets in, the reality of death sets in. The hero falls, the camera moves in so the audience can see the light go from his eyes, and the cigarette drops from his lips.

Do not turn your head away. Do not avert your gaze. This is a little like watching the sex act, is it not? The tension mounts, one stroke follows another, over and over again, and then there comes the consummation. Admit it, this hero's death is a giddy, intimate, ecstatic moment. This shop-worn scene is, undeniably, a romantic twist on the reality of battle, but I am not denigrating it for being cheesy. It can be, but that would be up to the writer and the director. This, or something similar, is the venerable climatic scene of dozens of war films, some of them great movies. I am not suggesting that this scene should not consummate your tale. Rather, I am trying to get at why it is venerable. Set it up well, it will deliver again and again. But the meaning is not in the action. The meaning, rather, is in what lies behind the action, what is within the hero.

I would go so far as to suggest that the war and romance genres are two sides of one coin. In both, Thanatos and Eros must resolve themselves in each other. If not, the book is not worth the reading; the movie is not worth the watching. It is irrelevant how much graphic sex or graphic violence is contained therein. All dramatic devices serve the same master.

This is why, in Act II of your war story, you probably should not be flashing back and forth between opposites –the seductress Eros and the seducer, Thanatos. That would be melodramatic. Focus rather on the chain that binds them together. Zoom in on the paradox.

It is unlikely that Thanatos would play as prominent a role in your story as he does in Shakespeare's Romeo and Juliet. In that play, the plot device of dual suicides, which is the romantic climax, is in danger of being over the top. But it is not over the top, because the great Bard knows a thing or two about how to craft a story. **You too will need to come up with something that does the job –something that adds shadow to your light– to render your story in three dimensions as opposed to what occurs in a melodrama.**

Art can only reflect and amplify aspects of the real, and Thanatos and Eros are at play, and at war, within us all. A romance story emphasizes Eros and a war story emphasizes Thanatos. I think that is fair. Keep in mind, though, that with birth comes the gift of life, as well as the gift of death. It is a paradox. You cannot have one without the other. Both are in every one of us. That was Freud's point.

As I said, romance and war are two sides of one coin. Romance speaks to the fusion of the emotional, physical, and spiritual, depicting the female force in its glorious, if potentially deadly, natural element. Every successful romance obliterates something, just as every successful blood-and-guts war story gives life to something. You might say that to write a war story, you turn a romance on its head, and vice-versa. War stories are obsessed with the obliteration of dragons, and, similar to the physics process of nuclear fission, draw energy from the separation of the emotional, the physical, and the spiritual. Both genres test the animal who is at odds with the spiritual, and convey what that implies about the mortal human journey.

For all fiction, the job is to lay bare the truth, happy or sad, ugly or beautiful, or something in between; and make some sense out of them. The best stories bring those seemingly discordant elements of life together into one harmonious chord in Act III. That is sometimes referred to as a feel-good story, and a few of them really are wonderful. (Example: It's A Wonderful Life.) The conceit of the storyteller is not that he or she has insight into the truth to convey, because that is simply the job description. The conceit is that this insight, once conveyed, can set us a little free from what encumbers our happiness. The truth will not free us from death or all suffering; but we can, at least, gain a glimpse of what the truth can do for us –what is truly valuable between the moment when we pass out of our mother's womb, through the various stages of life in Act II, and finally to Act III, where we settle back into the womb of the Earth mother.

You probably need both flavors as you cook your soup, but it is Eros trumping Thanatos for the romance genre, and usually the opposite in the war genre. The paradox is that, for both to work their magic, each must contain a measure of its opposite. For a war tale, the attraction of death, and the simultaneous attempt to defy death, must be present; and that should be felt viscerally in the audience as tension between the life force, Eros, and the death force, Thanatos.

The truth is that if you want to rivet your audience into those seats, it is an absolute requirement that your war story conveys love, or better yet even, a celebration of life. An example is the joyful family wedding at the beginning of Michael Cimino's Oscar-winning Vietnam War movie, The Deer Hunter.

The opposite is true for a romance. It cannot be just meadows and sunshine. The image of the bride, dressed in white, being swept off her feet and carried over the threshold in the strong manly arms of her "true love" happens in movies, but also in life. Remember the moment in Gone With The Wind when the strong-headed, vivacious redhead, Scarlet O'Hara, is swept off her feet by her dashing Rhett Butler, and carried up the stairs? My point is, death overwhelms life, but, in the romantic moment, life triumphs over death. You do not, in a romance story, just fall in love; in almost all romance stories you "surrender" to love. The concept of surrender is key here. When you surrender, something is lost. Here we have Thanatos taking the round from Eros. It is the circle of life. And so it goes.

Leaving aside the socialized aspect of gender roles, the storyteller must also surrender, in this case, to the fact that you can take the audience elsewhere, but you need first to go to where they are. Say what you want about where the audience should be, but even though Gone With The Wind is problematic from a modern audience's perspective –especially where race and gender are concerned– the audience, in 1939 on the eve of the USA entering World War II, was swept off of their collective feet.

Most people live their lives largely, if not completely, within their assigned social roles. What is that life, in terms of romance? At its locus are two people in love, with great hope, great joy, and with Thanatos being ushered over the bridal threshold. When a woman has a baby, she surrenders to the life force, placing her own life in peril to usher new life into the great wide world. When the baby arrives, both parents redefine themselves and their priorities and step out of their self-centered roles. In a sense, they sacrifice their lives, which is Thanatos. Despite variations, most people follow the script. Whether the author is nature or nurture, both are fascinating and important, but that is not what is at issue here. What is relevant is that on this stage and acting within this script, most of us love and live.

As for a war story, the more passionate the love (in this context, love between fellow soldiers) the more the writer earns the ultra-violence. For romance, the more your story surrenders to the shadow of Thanatos –even as you pay homage to the light of Eros– the more you access universal truth. At the heart of romance, the self collides with the selfless. There is love that blinds, love that knocks you to the ground, love that changes and informs you; but there is also love that requires the surrender of much of what has so far defined you and seems to transcend any socialization. What follows is the most famous speech from Shakespeare's *As You Like It*. Aspiring storytellers, please pay close attention:

> *All the world's a stage,*
> *And all the men and women merely players;*
> *They have their exits and their entrances,*
> *And one man in his time plays many parts,*
> *His acts being seven ages. At first, the infant,*
> *Mewling and puking in the nurse's arms.*
> *Then the whining schoolboy, with his satchel*
> *And shining morning face, creeping like a snail*

Unwillingly to school. And then the lover,
Sighing like a furnace, with a woeful ballad
Made to his mistress' eyebrow. Then a soldier,
Full of strange oaths and bearded like the pard,
Jealous in honor, sudden and quick in quarrel,
Seeking the bubble reputation
Even in the cannon's mouth. And then the justice,
In fair round belly with good capon lined,
With eyes severe and beard of formal cut,
Full of wise saws and modern instances;
And so he plays his part. The sixth age shifts
Into the lean and slippered pantaloon,
With spectacles on nose and pouch on side;
His youthful hose, well saved, a world too wide
For his shrunk shank, and his big manly voice,
Turning again toward childish treble, pipes
And whistles in his sound. Last scene of all,
That ends this strange eventful history,
Is second childishness and mere oblivion,
Sans teeth, sans eyes, sans taste, sans everything.

In Act I of a well-crafted war movie, there will probably be a scene or two about passion and the love of life. Sometimes that scene will be a flashback. Typically, the soldier will be seen leaving behind his wife, who stands on the porch of the farmhouse, watching him go, struggling to smile. There is an American flag in the shot. Then...

CLOSING IN on: Wife. A tear falling.

P.O.V. Wife: (point of view shot). Soldier walks out of the gateway with his rucksack heaved across his broad back. He looks back.

LONG: Wife waving goodbye.

This scene, or something like it, is there to remind the audience about what is worth fighting for –i.e. flag and family. These kinds of scenes are necessary because well-crafted war movies are not just about the joy of blowing up things or people –although, I must admit, I too take some guilty pleasure in this. **What is more compelling to me, however, as a storyteller and mov-iemaker, is how almost everything important and precious comes into focus within the perilous fog of war.**

It should surprise no one when the males in the audi-ence are riveted to the screen during a battle scene as things go boom and limbs are ripped off bodies, their female companions are looking away. Comrades in arms become real to each other when in battle, and the men in the audience become more real to themselves when watching a battle. The point is that males too are looking for insight into who and what they are, what their true purpose is, and how best to conduct their lives so that happiness is maximized. It is just that different demo-graphics go for different bait.

Women, in our society anyway, still seem to be more comfortable opening up to each other. Men, not so much. Males often require an intermediary, such as sports or automobiles, to talk about their emotions, but they ad-dress the issue sidewise like a crab. Many males prefer a metaphor to direct confrontation with that dragon. When it concerns their emotional needs –which, after all, are the prime motivators for both males and fe-males– men are often at sea. Revelations on the emo-tional front, which might seem ho-hum obvious to fe-males who spend more of their time with their lives and relationships exposed to each other, can have great sig-nificance to males. It seems to me that men have no less need for what has been called "emotional intelligence" than do women. Perhaps how they address that need is the difference.

As an emotionally stunted young male myself, David Lean's great war epic, Lawrence Of Arabia, was formative for me. Lean's next Oscar-winning romantic movie, Doctor Zhivago, a wonderful romance story, was not nearly as significant. So be it. To each their own, as the farmer said, as he kissed his cow goodnight.

None of this should be contentious. **In war movies, the revelation and testing of character is what entertains the target audience.** What might appear to some media critics as pandering to prurient male blood lust may be, in fact, be addressing quite different needs. If you ask me why Steven Spielberg's Saving Private Ryan was so successful at the box office, I will tell you it was because it brought the male-skewed audience to themselves. **There is a human need –not a male need, not a female need – to separate the signal from the noise, and the war movie is just one means to this end.**

Nevertheless, we refer to Universal Themes or Universal Truths. There are no gender-specific Universal Truths. The truths illuminated in a war story or a romance story are equally universal. At core, what is important is the same to males and to females. You can see the truth of that contention when a movie does not come gender/genre labeled. (In Hollywood, they call that a "crossover" film.) Make one of the central protagonists a woman, and many more women will watch a war movie, as long as it reveals and tests character. (Case in point: Zero Dark Thirty). Make a romance a comedy that accomplishes almost exactly the same ends, except do not market it as a rom-com, and millions of guys will see it, enjoy it, and talk about it over a beer (The 40-Year-Old Virgin).

22. Fiction Versus Nonfiction: A False Dichotomy

What sets apart a work of fiction from an essay, documentary, or academic paper is not that one is a work of the imagination and the other real. All good fiction and nonfiction is rooted in what is real. All require an exercise of the imagination; all require logic and empirical knowledge. An essay or an academic paper, however, is not a story. Rather, it is an argument to prove the facts –done artfully, one hopes– but it not as art. All documentaries and works of fiction are stories and, therefore, works of art. They are siblings. Those others are more distant relatives.

Both documentaries and fictional narrative movies are theme-driven and set within a three act structure. They share the same storytelling rules. A documentary, however, is a document of something that happened. The situations in a document are real, not contrived. There is an attempt to portray something that actually happened as it really happened –as a document. That is the prime distinction between fiction filmmaking and documentary making, but because a documentary is also a story, not just a record, "why" it happened drives the entire project, just as it does for a work of fiction. Why this happened still needs to be illuminated, even if it is happening right in front of the camera in real time, as can be seen in cinéma vérité style documentaries.

On the other side of the ledger, for fiction, when imaginary characters are placed in challenging, imaginary situations, what is imagined nevertheless needs to be predicated on real life situations, or the fictional story will fail.

Someone I know, who has made both documentaries and fictional narrative films, described the different process-es to me. Shooting a documentary is like playing jazz in a small ensemble, with what is unfolding in front of the camera leading, and the filmmakers improvising. Fic-tional movie making is more like being in an orchestra playing classical music, with the music laid out before you, and what happens in front of the camera governed mostly by what is indicated in the notation.

As in life, as in art. As in art, as in life. It is another dialectic with fiction making and non-fiction docu-mentary making, cycling in opposite directions but accomplishing essentially the same thing.

In any competent fiction, universal themes are set inside a human skin, and played out between protagonists and antagonists in situations where making the right choices are major challenges. This is as true for science fiction or superhero fantasies as it is for any other fictional narra-tive genre. In Act II, it does not matter if protagonists can fly, time-travel, or if they possess superhuman strength. The choices presented by the antagonists might be exag-gerated from what normally confronts mere mortals like us, but they are based on what people in the audience face in their real lives every day. **How these challeng-es are met by protagonists, and how they respond, is how you and I might respond, albeit probably in less fanciful situations. The psychology in the story must echo our own. War or romance, comedy or tragedy, all genres are just amplifiers of life as we know it**. We borrow the Greek term "drama" because fiction ampli-fies. Even so, documentary storytelling and narrative fictional storytelling are far more similar than they are different.

It is unlikely that anyone in the audience will be facing a fire-breathing dragon anytime soon, but a dragon of a boss can suffice as the antagonistic force in a work of narrative fiction or in a documentary. The connection to the audience's experiences must be visceral for both, and the tales told in both need to be constructed to meet the audience's interests and needs. **If the audience you are writing for is not facing something similar to what you depict in fiction, they will not be interested. The same goes for a documentary.**

23. Simplifying, Exaggerating, And Making Things Up

No matter how complex or nuanced a particular story might be, storytelling involves simplification and exaggeration. Real life is the model, even for fantasy, but real life needs to be filtered and amplified for a story. The same can be said of your characters and the situations you throw them into in Act II. They will have to be simplified and exaggerated, but these will be simplifications and exaggerations from real life. There are two prime reasons for this:

1. We do not possess omniscience. We cannot replicate life and when we try, the result is dead on the page or screen. The words "art," "artificial" and "artifice" are related for this reason. It is the best we can manage.

2. Exaggeration and simplification are necessary devices, and help the audience focus on what is important. Separating the signal from the noise is the job, but sometimes what is signal to one person is background noise to another. No matter how rigorous our efforts

to be objective, humans –including scientists, and even judges– are condemned to being subjective. Our keenest insights are colored and distorted by our psychology. It is just that some insights are less limited than others are. We need to be honest with ourselves about our own range of insight and expertise. Simplifying, in that sense, is another way of saying "Write what you know."

Every storyteller who has developed the mettle to succeed has made the choice to be honest. I do not mean honesty about anything and everything, but two orders of honesty are required: self-honesty, and honesty with your readers or audience. It is not necessary to be honest with spouses or creditors, but it is usually a good idea. Writers are not required to be saints. Writers are not even required to be especially good people, except in the ways delineated above.

Not being remotely a saint actually can work to a writer's advantage. You can write firsthand with personal insight and honesty about what it is like to experience failure, moral weakness, unseemliness, humiliation, and defeat. You can write about serious character flaws from your own experience, if you are honest and courageous enough. Your writing will always be but a pale reflection of a small portion of what is. That is a given. But do it anyway. Specialize, focus on what you think you know, exaggerate it and simplify it. If you have done your homework, your insights will resonate in the relatively small portion of humanity that is your audience or readership.

That a fiction writer can really only write about him or herself has become a cliché, but like most clichés, there is some truth in it. But from the writer's point of view, the pursuit of what it is like to be human is the meat, and most of this book has parsed out what that statement implies. Simplifying is rarely easy. Exaggeration is often too easy. You need to simplify and exaggerate to get at what is important about being a human. Both the art and the craft of this profession require insight into what it means to be human. Daffy Duck is but a human in duck drag. Daffy informs us about aspects of ourselves. And, yes, we seem to need an outside agency, in this case the storytelling team that created those marvelous cartoons, to connect the dots for us about ourselves. Odd, but that is only human.

Human skins are sensitive and vulnerable, unlike the thick-scaled skins of dragons. To wear a human skin is often to be uncomfortable, oversensitive, uncertain, contradictory, envious, spiteful, violent, and terrified. Demons penetrate our thin skins and employ our human weaknesses to torment us, and that torment can and usually does result in neuroses. It is our own neurosis and our inner demons that often cause us to make poor choices, like a betrayal, or a little murder. But these demons can be identified and classified and formed into antagonists that act on protagonists. The human neuroses burbling inside us can be explained, exploited, exposed, and distilled into great writing about us, about human psychology.

The challenge is to know what to emphasize and place at center-stage, and what to leave off stage altogether –not even if it might also be important and true, but especially because it is also important and true. It dilutes your storytelling. It throws your Act II off-track. It is fatal to tell too many stories at once. You do not have the capacity. Simplify and exaggerate. Do that in the full knowledge that every personality is endlessly nuanced, every life is larded with multi-layered contradiction and paradox, and that that is also how life is experienced. **Experience,** however, is not a story. Life is a series of events, which is also not a story. Stories are stories. Stories inform us about life. Stories lay bare our themes. That is their purpose.

CONCLUSION

You, poor scribe, will need to draw on your meager insight to shine a light into the mess that is yourself, and us. You will need to shine a light, but that light will not always be sunshine. Sometimes it will be moonlight. Sometimes it will be but a match-light flaring in the shadow, illuminating only for a second, and that will have to be illumination enough. Sometimes, though, the light you shine will be like the harsh, blinding, cold blue lights set over an operating table, and you will be both the surgeon and the patient, laid out on the operating table.

It is quite a trick to possess both the steady-handed arrogance of a surgeon and the vulnerable humility of the patient. Mostly, though, it is humility that you require. You require humility to count yourself in amongst the flawed, scared, cowed, sentient, highly sensitive, stubborn, paradoxical creatures that we are. This requires brutal self-honesty, which rarely comes easy, but is an achievement. The unexamined life may, indeed, be a life not worth living, but all that internal exploration can leave you irritable, irascible, depressed, raw and driven to drink or drugs. Remember, too much pot spoils the cook. Pull yourself up. Never forget who you are.

You are being inducted into the Order of the Magi. Don your top hat, cape, and tails before you mount the stage. You must draw yourself out of wherever you are to appear bold and imposing in top hat, cape, and tails. This is you in your starring role, as trickster, as magician. And here you are, waving your wand, creating illusions that are at once trick and truth. **You will need to learn whatever you must learn to master the trick of simplifying and exaggerating, to separate the signal from the noise, and coalesce, out of what seems to be thin air, the magical bit of artifice that is the story well told.**